My Muslir

Communicating well with your Muslim friend

Stafford Allen

GILEAD
B O O K S
PUBLISHING

Gilead Books Publishing
Corner Farm
West Knapton
Malton
North Yorkshire YO17 8JB UK
www.GileadBooksPublishing.com

First published in Great Britain, September 2016
2 4 6 8 10 9 7 5 3 1

British Library Cataloguing-in-Publication Data:
A catalogue record for this book is available from the British
Library.

ISBN: 978-0-9932090-6-2

The publisher makes every effort to ensure that the papers used
in our books are made from trees that have been legally sourced
from well-managed and credibly certified forests by using a
printer awarded FSC & PEFC chain of custody certification.

Cover design: Nathan Ward
Cover image: ©Deanpictures | Dreamstime.com

Contents

Foreword

Islam and Muslims hit the headlines these days. Church seminars about Islam attract many more attendants than parallel meetings on other topics. Christians are perplexed about what to believe about Islam. They are caught between the politically correct teaching that violent Islamists are not truly Muslim and are a small minority, and that true Islam is a religion of peace which also has love of neighbour as its goal; and on the other hand the prevalence of terrorist violence within Muslim communities around the world and horrendous persecution of Christians and other non-Muslims by those who call themselves Muslims.

When we read the Qur'an, we find verses which advocate a friendly relationship with Jews and Christians, who are commended as People of the Book. These are generally early revelations, from the period when Mohammed was still in Mecca. We also discover less attractive verses, which recommend unloving violence towards Christians and Jews. The Muslim doctrine of abrogation means that the later revelations supersede the earlier ones - a major issue for more moderate Muslims.

Stafford Allen's book helps us not only with the issue of Muslim violence, but also opens up to us the attitudes and understandings of the ordinary Muslims we may meet in everyday life at work, college or on the street. He is looking at what they feel and believe at 'gut' level. Inevitably the Muslims we meet will tend to be largely more moderate, for the Islamists are often unwilling to relate to other people. Stafford Allen has a rich background experience, having lived for many years in various Muslim countries and working as a doctor in a largely Pakistani Muslim city community in Britain.

This book is delightfully written, very informative and very helpful for Christians with the opportunity of sharing their faith with Muslims around them. When you have read it, pass it on!

Martin Goldsmith
All Nations Christian College
Ware, England

Preface

It is a great sadness that I cannot, in the present climate, mention people by name, and so all names have been changed and locations have been disguised. I cannot emphasise enough how much I owe to all those whom I have had the joy of working alongside, from whom I have learned so much, and who have put up with my mistakes. Personal as this book is, I hope it will become clear as you read on how much I owe to others and how team work is everything.

All the episodes and conversations are faithfully recorded, with the exception of 'A cautionary tale' in Chapter 1, which is of course fiction, as is the parable of the Roundians and Squarians in Chapter 8.

I have kept footnotes to a minimum but there is an extensive booklist at the back, with a 'top 10' for those overwhelmed by its length.

Stafford Allen
September 2016

Introduction

If you had asked me if I was a Christian during the first two decades of my life I would have answered "yes" without hesitation. Brought up in a Church of England family and environment, I went to school and heard the Bible read every day. The services were short and lively, if traditional, and I was confirmed at the age of 14. I was surrounded by a Christian culture and it was comfortable in every way. When I left school the fun, business and excitement of life as an army officer pushed any thoughts of God into the background.

Then something happened which was to change my life forever. I was taken to the ballroom of the Kensington Palace Hotel, and there, in a meeting held by City Christians, I encountered God in a terrifyingly real way. Without any kind of 'churchiness' or Christian jargon, the Good News about Christ was explained. At least I was told that it was; I remember nothing of what was said, only a huge inner conflict. In a moment all the wallpaper of my early life suddenly became real and three-dimensional. Jesus was alive and he was there. In my confusion I had nothing to say but "yes".

On the way home I confided to James, the friend who had taken me, that I felt entirely and utterly different.

Over the next few days things fell into place. I realised that I had 'become a Christian'. I had an extraordinary sense of God's presence. This was confirmed in practical terms when, two days later, I was released entirely from smoking, something I had made many futile attempts to achieve.

It strikes me that the experience of many Muslims is not too far from my own. Brought up and taught about an integrated faith and worldview, it is comfortable: it is what everyone around accepts. Nothing from outside challenges its rightness. It is more than right, it is *what is.*

My wife and I have worked with Muslim people for more than three decades in a variety of contexts. My wife has been a Bible translator and home maker, a theology teacher in churches and theological colleges, a counsellor and a lecturer. She has cooked, cleaned, walked many miles visiting the sick and comforting the bereaved with Jordanian, Sudanese and British fellow church workers. I have worked as doctor in primary health care, tuberculosis treatment and control, prison medicine and general practice. We have worked with Muslim people in a wide variety of situations; with nomads in Sudan, Palestinians in Jordan and Kashmiris in the UK.

During this time there have been massive changes. More than at any time in history, Muslim people have been becoming disciples and followers of Jesus. Although in some countries they are numerically small, proportionally the growth of churches from Muslim background believers has been hugely significant. In Algeria, Indonesia and Iran, large numbers of men and women have become Christians. At the same time there has been a marked change in attitude among Christians in the West and, perhaps more importantly, amongst many Christians in the ancient churches in the Middle East; Muslims are no longer seen as somehow unable to hear and believe the Christian message. Work among Muslims is accepted as part of mainline Christian mission. These changes have taken place in a politically volatile climate. The War on Terror has come, and it seems, gone. British troops are serving in Muslim countries. The Arab Spring has come and turned to autumn. Syria is being ripped apart by ISIS and its own rulers. Old borders, imposed by colonial powers, are being torn up and redrawn. ISIS and other versions of Islam are fighting a civil war within Islam itself.

Political change has been paralleled by social revolution and geographical upheaval. Large numbers of Muslim people have settled in all the larger cities of Britain and Europe and have had families that have grown up as part of our society. New migrants and refugees arrive daily. Few non-Muslims do not have a Muslim acquaintance at school, work, or as a neighbour. In many areas 'ethnic minorities' have become local majorities.

Looking back over my experience of this exciting and fascinating period, I can see that I have learned slowly and with many mistakes. I recall many painful episodes where my well-meaning efforts to discuss the Christian Good News with Muslims were thrown back in my face or just seemed irrelevant. I was forced to reflect deeply on how the Gospel could and should be effectively communicated. Surely God's word is for everyone equally? The result is this book. There are plenty of new mistakes to make; why go on making all the old ones? The principles I have set out are extraordinarily simple, not to say obvious. But they did not always seem so to me. They are certainly not my own discovery and I claim no originality. Nor are they in any way a technique or a solution. 'Preaching the Gospel' always seems to be about the agony and the ecstasy, the many tears and struggles – and moments of pure joy and delight.

This book is not really about Islam. It is much more about Muslim people; the men and women around us. I am writing for those who, having Muslim friends and colleagues, would like a little help in reaching them with the Christian message in a way that is understandable and accessible. It is not a 'how to' book; in fact, the opposite. Throughout, the emphasis is 'ask and find out' rather than 'do it this way', and you will certainly not see a string of spectacular results recorded in these pages. My aim is to help people escape from preconceptions that cause anxiety and sometimes paralysis. Muslims are in many ways different but in so many ways exactly the same as ourselves. If your response is 'but I can do *that*'; if I can help you to discover that Muslims, far from being difficult and sensitive are often far more easy to share your faith with than your twenty-first century secular friends; if I can help you find out that talking about Jesus to Muslim people can be fun and exciting, then I will have succeeded. If your response is 'well I knew that already' it will only prove that these ideas are far from new.

This book will be most useful for those living in Britain amongst people who originate from the Middle East and the Asian subcontinent, but I hope very much that it will be helpful and stimulating for others.

I start with an attempt to replace one paradigm with another. The idea that 'Islam is a strong religion that is believed by people and communities and whole countries. It has a powerful hold over them. This makes them hard to share the Good News with, but if I study Islam carefully I will be better equipped to reach them,' is replaced with 'My friend, his family and the people in his street live their lives within a strong belief framework that affects them socially, politically, emotionally and spiritually at a very deep level and results in a particular worldview. If I observe my friend, get to know him well, spend time with him, form a real relationship, and ask him about these things, I will understand him better and be better equipped to share the Good News of Christ in a language he can understand.'

This approach has the advantage of centring our attention on the person and on the present situation. It means that we are honouring our friend by trying to find out the truth about him or her rather than studying what he or she should, (but may well not) believe.

I follow this with a variety of cultural signposts. Many of these, such as the Prophet, the Qur'an, and the veil, are well-explained elsewhere in terms of more formal Muslim belief and practice; my purpose is to look at these through emotional, anthropological and cultural eyes rather than doctrinal ones, and to help the reader use them as stepping stones to his or her own quest to know and understand the person or community they are engaging with. If we are looking to understand our friend and the way he or she thinks, we need to be aware of a number of features of his or her culture that will help us as we seek to understand him. These are there as guidelines to our tactful enquiry about how he or she functions, both as an individual and as a family member.

Then come a few more features to look out for and to appreciate, as factors that make it easier to make genuine contact with Muslims now than ever before, as well as some stumbling blocks and difficulties.

The second part of the book is devoted to exploring ways of 'sharing the Gospel' in a non-Western but entirely biblical way by means of presence, work, prayer, our own story of our life with God, and the scriptures, and showing how differently these are seen and experienced by Muslims in comparison with post-Christian Western people.

Much of this book centres on 'language', what our words convey or what emotional response they elicit; what misunderstandings they convey - or worse, cover. There is more of this later, but I have already used technical language or jargon. What do I mean by 'Christian,' 'mission,' 'Gospel,' or 'Muslim'?

As for 'Christian,' if you like the cap, wear it. However, I am writing for those who will take the same line as the football coach who, when accused of treating his sport as though it was a matter of life and death, replied that of course it wasn't - it was far more serious than that!

Mission? This is the church and the individual sharing the Good News in practical and verbal form, showing love, courage and sensitivity to men and women who are not 'Christians'.

Gospel? A good English word that should be used and properly understood rather than discarded, and I have used it alternately alongside 'Good News'. This is not the formula that it has on occasion been reduced to, but rather the spoken and lived truth about Jesus as found in the Bible in its full sense, with its political, social, personal and collective dimensions all expressed in a culturally understandable way. More - the Good News is not just about Jesus; it *is* Jesus. The medium is the message.

'Muslim'? If my friend calls him or herself one that is good enough for me.

My other reasons for writing are simpler. I would like to set down some of our many experiences of God in the tiny corners of his world that we have been assigned to. This journey has been shared with many dear friends, and I owe them thanks for many joys and sorrows shared. I have learned so much and benefitted so deeply from the worldwide fellowship of Christian men and women on the 'mission field'.

Finally, I am writing because of the deepest and most undeserved privilege of all; we have known God.

Chapter 1

Theologians

A cautionary tale

Ahmed, a young and dedicated imam, is graduating from the Al-Azhar Mosque University in Cairo, the epicentre of learning in the Muslim world. As he walks out of the gates for the last time clutching his coveted certificate as a theologian and teacher of Islam, Ahmed is considering what God wants him to do with his knowledge and training. He sits drinking sweet mint tea in a crowded and noisy restaurant. Contemplating his next step, Ahmed is convinced that he should go to England and convert the English to Islam.

From his school days Ahmed has learned that Britain is a Christian country. Being a conscientious young man, he knows that he must study Christianity before venturing abroad. He puts down his empty tea glass, pays the bill, jumps onto a bus and makes his way to a library. For the next three months Ahmed studies the writings of Calvin and Luther as well as Karl Barth and the more modern theologians. He reads the Book of Common Prayer, carefully noting important aspects of Church history and Christian doctrine. He reads the Bible.

Finally Ahmed feels that he is adequately prepared to encounter the British; he understands something of their religion and hence the way they think. Soon he arrives in Sheffield.

Imagine the shock of the poor man as he encounters Wayne on the no. 52 Bus. Wayne is every inch a secular twenty-first century young man. He knows that the Bible exists but has never read it; it is totally irrelevant to his life. The Book of Common Prayer? It is in funny language and belongs far back in the past. He has heard dimly of Calvin. And Luther, wasn't that the guy who had a lot to do with black Americans in the US Deep South? But as for Karl Barth - who on earth is he for goodness sake?

Where did Ahmed go wrong? He has made the assumption that studying Christianity will help him to understand the people in a 'Christian' country. The label 'Christian' turns out to be wholly misleading. What he has studied so carefully may be what theologians and Bible students study in universities, but if Ahmed thinks that his newfound knowledge of 'Christianity' will help him to understand the way Wayne and his secular friends think, he will get nowhere. He will fail to get under the skin of Wayne and those like him. It will be fortunate for Ahmed if he learns this lesson quickly.

Ahmed's wrong assumption is based on the belief that the disciplines of theology that stood him in such good stead in the study of his own religion will be equally useful when he comes to understanding someone else's faith. In fact they are almost useless, and even counter-productive.

Of course this story is fiction, and perhaps rather exaggerated, but it illustrates the trap that Christians can easily fall into out of the best motives. We feel that we need to understand those whom we are trying to contact with God's love, and we do! But as we go about it we can make some seriously wrong assumptions: that when we study Islam it will lead to an understanding of the Muslim men and women we meet and seek to get to know; that the same tried and tested methods of study with which we are familiar as Christians will be the right ones with which to study Islam; and that through this study, we have arrived at an understanding of our Muslim friends. We will be fortunate if, like Ahmed, we discover early on that we are not on the right track.

This is not to say that theology is not a vital science; it is. It is the nervous system of the Church, and of the individual disciple of Jesus. It is there for our nourishment and enjoyment, and a Christian without theology is severely handicapped and vulnerable. All I am saying is that the art and science of theology is not the right tool for the job we are embarking on, just as nuclear physics does not help you understand medieval paintings, and podiatry is no help when it comes to hairdressing.

This is not the only false assumption that we have to correct. Ahmed comes from a pre-Enlightenment culture that is seamlessly integrated in a way that Western culture has not been since the middle ages. Islam is to him the all-encompassing world in which he lives: it is the context of his social life, politics, history, family life, language, the way he looks at the world, the way he looks out of his own world into your world 'outside', as well as of his formal beliefs and what he does in the mosque on Friday. He does not divide his life into compartments. When Ahmed says "I wear Muslim clothes on Friday," I might murmur to myself "He means Arab clothes..." - but he doesn't! Ahmed is telling me that even the clothing he wears to the mosque is Islamic. I should listen to him. Theological disciplines will not by themselves unlock the door of Ahmed's world.

My suggestion is that we cease to look at Islam from a purely theological perspective - as religion - but as a 'biosphere,' in which culture, law, politics, history, tradition, family life, earthly worldview and view of the hidden but ever-present spiritual world are all seamlessly woven together. Islamic religion, with its Prophet, its practices, its book and its language, is the central and unifying feature of this biosphere, which has very marked frontiers to the world outside, but whose interior features diversity and conflict.

This indicates a pre-Enlightenment worldview, and the Islamic biosphere is characterised by pre-Enlightenment, or medieval, thinking; by which I mean a culture that is characterised by a reverence for and acceptance of authority, an educational philosophy that is concerned with absorbing and transmitting a body of knowledge, rather than with experiment and free enquiry, an outlook that strongly emphasises the corporate rather than the individual, where 'role' is more important than 'identity'. Democracy, free speech and the spirit of free enquiry have no particular value.

This contrasts with the outlook that has prevailed in the West since the seventeenth- and eighteenth-century Enlightenment. Authority is more and more called into question and is more and more subject to criticism.

Education, as well as being about absorbing 'knowledge,' is about free enquiry, open questioning and criticism from which no authority, however respected, is exempt. There is a strong, almost exclusive, emphasis on the individual and their personal potential. Free speech and democracy are expressly valued.

It follows that there are profound differences and contrasts between our cultures which may be unrecognised, but which will lead to constant confusion when my Muslim neighbour and I try to relate to each other. So often we don't communicate or end up in conflict and we wonder why. It is because although we inhabit the same street we live in different biospheres.

With all this in mind, it is easier to appreciate that people are Muslims for many diverse reasons. Most are Muslims through birth and tradition; some because they cannot escape. Very many are Muslims because here is where their identity lies. They may hold firmly to the tenets of Islam but few will have arrived at their belief through earnest enquiry or searching.

There is a process in which Muslim societies in Britain are in many ways moving from a pre-Enlightenment outlook to a more post-Enlightenment one, while at the same time trying to defend it. The struggles of many individuals reflect this.

It also quickly becomes apparent that 'religion' is a very dangerous and misleading word that leads us to make connections that are quite unjustified, as we will see in Chapter 6.

Theology? Mind the gap!

As Christians we are all theologians. We read the Bible carefully, we read commentaries, and we also read theology. We do this so that we may grow as Christians. But if we are honest, we are all too well aware of the gap between what should be, and what actually is.

Here is an example. Jesus says in Matthew's Gospel:

> ...Do not worry about your life, what you will eat or what you will drink, or about your body, what you will wear...But seek first his kingdom and his righteousness, and all these things will be given to you as well. Therefore do not worry about tomorrow...(Matthew ch.6 v.25-34)

Do I believe this? Of course I do! I believe what Jesus says and I am convinced that he is reliable; that God is concerned about all my needs and I have no need to worry where the next meal is coming from. So...when I see the price of petrol going through the roof, and I contemplate the fact that I might not have a job in the next two months, why do I wake up at night sweating?

It is because what I believe in my head does not wholly control my life, much though I may want it to. I so much want to live my life by what Jesus says, but it is often a struggle!

If I believed perfectly, perhaps I would give away so much more money than I do now, and lie awake at night much less. My wife and I were members of a Christian organisation in which it was a bedrock principle that we should never ask for money and that we should rely on what Jesus has said about meeting all our needs. Sometimes it was exciting and stimulating. Sometimes it was a struggle, (especially for the accountants). No wonder the father of the epileptic boy burst out, "Lord I believe, help my unbelief." After many years it is still often difficult. Our daily lives and what we believe in our hearts are often far from what we sincerely say that we believe.

What should be is not always *what is*. To generalise horribly we may say that theology is the study of *what should be*. Islamic theology is no less *what should be* than its Christian counterpart, but when it comes to getting close to our Muslim friends and understanding the way they think, we are not at all interested in *what should be*. Instead, we are interested in *what is*. This is not theology at all; it is social anthropology! If someone wants to discover what I believe and what is going on deep down, he needs to be an anthropologist, not a theologian. The anthropologist is not the least bit interested in what should be - only in what is.

Picture what is going on by thinking of anatomy. We can imagine three parts of the body - head, heart, and gut - and, figuratively, see what is happening at each level. This is the same for all of us, whatever we believe, (or even if we profess to believe nothing), but here I am looking at it with our Muslim friends in mind.

The head

In the head are 'formal' beliefs and creeds; thoughts, analysis and argument. This is the level of consciously worked out theology and dogma. When as a good Anglican I say the Creed in a church service, starting with "I believe..." this comes from my head, the conscious part of my brain where I formulate beliefs. Your Muslim friend may have very strongly and sincerely-held beliefs at this level, and may articulate them forcefully to you. This is the level where we often get stuck in a discussion and we wonder why things have gone badly. Anyone who has spent any time working with Muslims will have experienced the 'head banger', the bruising encounter, the one-sided conversation where your friend has done nearly all the talking and you have come away battered and feeling rather defeated. Much Islamic doctrine and belief may have been thrown at you, nearly all of which you may already know. It is the area of *what should be.*

Why has this happened? It is because Islam is very strong in the 'head' area. Great emphasis is placed on Islamic doctrine. Mothers teach their children about Islam; later the children often go to mosque school, where there is virtually no discussion, and Islam is taught as a body of knowledge. The concern is not intellectual or spiritual growth, but that the correct body of knowledge is taken on board. In Britain these schools are often modeled on schools in the home country, where education is by rote. For someone who has experienced a Western education it is hardly possible to imagine what goes on there, but those who attend these schools are never taught how to ask questions or share knowledge. Pause a moment while you walk past a mosque school and listen, or even better, ask someone to invite you to attend an evening's teaching; you will hear a great deal of rote learning and group recitation and very little else. Even if your Muslim friend has been to a European school and is an electronics graduate she will have learned Islam in this way in the mosque. It follows that at the 'head' level, it is unlikely that a Muslim will be able to discuss her religion and her belief with you in a way that your own education has prepared you for. Your Muslim friend's way of 'preaching' to you (or at you) is far more to do with the education that he or she has been subjected to than what you might feel is personal obstinacy, rudeness or 'spiritual hardness'.

This is also the area where we are divided by pre- and post-Enlightenment thinking. We in the West take for granted the right to challenge all authorities and experts, and in turn they themselves expect to be challenged and held to account for their opinions and judgements. Islamic thinking is the opposite. Muslims do not challenge the received wisdom of their scholars. This is why Western reasoning often fails. Our careful and seemingly irrefutable arguments are ineffectual, to our confusion. Why? Because your friend's acceptance of authority, which to him is a virtue, renders him impervious to your reasoning.

The 'head' level is also the level of the 'persona', the image of the kind of person that you consciously want people to think you are. Because Islam is a religion of shame and honour it may be very important to your Muslim friend that he or she is seen to be a good and devout Muslim, not only in front of his family and friends, but also in your eyes. This will strongly influence the way he or she talks to you about Islam. The bruising-encounter conversation may take place with others present, in which case you may well be used by your friends in a show-match that is set up to demonstrate to each other what good Muslims they all are. Of course this is not a conscious arrangement, but it is an unhealthy situation for both you and your Muslim friends and should be avoided. It is one of the reasons why one-to-one encounters are usually freer from such agendas, and tend to be so much more productive.

The heart

Figuratively this is the home of the emotions. Islam is sometimes pictured as grave and dignified, and in some senses it is. However, we will never understand our Muslim friends unless we see Islam's very powerful emotional side. Try to get an invitation to attend the Prophet's birthday celebration; your Muslim friend will be only too delighted to take you. You will enjoy the party atmosphere, the feasting and jollity, the many stalls selling books and DVDs about the Prophet and his wonderful life. You might also go to a recitation of the Qur'an with your friend. The intonation and the unique manner of the recitation is a special skill, and a good reader will move his hearers deeply; you may hear gasps of joy and ecstasy.

What is going on here? When did you last hear groans from the congregation when the Bible was read in church? It is at the 'heart' level that the deep love for the Prophet Muhammad is found which is a major feature of Islamic religion for so many people. It will not often be articulated and certainly never in the way that 'head' dogma is expounded, but it is a vital part of Islamic life and belief. It is there to be observed and appreciated by those who have eyes to see.

The gut

As we move further and deeper inwards, we come finally to the area that we are trying to reach. We have arrived at the level of *what is.* Here in the gut are the beliefs that we do not articulate, and whose existence we may not even recognise. Here are the family influences, the deep hopes and aspirations, as well as the fears. Here are the beliefs that actually motivate our lives and make us act like we do. In our normal relationships we gradually and naturally move to this level with people we trust, and we need to equip ourselves to move to this level with our Muslim friends.

You may well find that there are assumptions and beliefs held by your Muslim friend that are not related to Islam at all. It is here that the magic and occult that is such a feature of Islam in so many countries is found; this tends to motivate people's lives in a way that theological Islam can never do. Without recognizing this, our picture of our Muslim friends will be incomplete, our relationships will be shallow, and our opportunity to share the Good News will be prejudiced.

Fortunately there are uncomplicated ways of making contact beyond the 'head' level, through the 'heart' level and onto the 'gut' level. These ways allow us to open our eyes and begin to explore at least some parts of the Islamic biosphere, and the hearts, minds and lives of our Muslim friends, and to appreciate the pre-Enlightenment mindset that is so different from our own. We will outline some of these in the next chapter.

We will be much better able to do that if we have had a good look at ourselves at this level first, because this model of 'head, heart and gut' is equally true for Christians (and for that matter people of all faiths and none). We must never fall into the trap of feeling that we are somehow special and that our minds do not work in this way. We need to have a long hard look at our own inconsistencies, at how our own faith in Christ is expressed in our heads, at how we enjoy the emotional side of our spiritual life, and at how it is translated into the gut-level engine room that truly runs our lives. How important is it to us that we seem 'good Christians' to our family and peers? What is our Christian emotional life like? What is really going on deep down - and is it consistent with what we believe in our heads?

Chapter 2

...or Anthropologists

I picked up a booklet in a hospital. It was entitled 'What Muslims Believe'. Containing a brief outline of Islamic belief and practice, it was there to help non-Muslim employees in the NHS understand their Muslim patients. It was a sincere attempt, but fell well into the category of 'theology' in the 'head' area. It showed no understanding of Muslim belief and practice as it really is.

When we embark on our quest to find out how Muslims 'tick', how to get down to the heart and from there to the gut, it is right to start by reading a good overview of Islam. We need to appreciate not only early Islamic history but also how Muslim politics and thought have developed over the past century or so to lead to present-day developments, how Islamic history is so built into the worldview of Muslims, and how this worldview is so radically different from our own. We must never neglect our homework. We need to read; we need to understand how Muslims see their own culture, religion and history. But this is only our starting point.

Fortunately we can narrow down our aim. It is a great relief to know that we do not have to understand 'Islam' or Muslim people in general, as if such a thing were possible. No, we are actually only concerned with understanding our Muslim colleague at work, the people in our street, the family next door, and the friend who we happen to be talking to at the moment. We can forget the entire rest of the Muslim world and concentrate on the unique, fascinating and very human people on our doorstep.

And how are we going to do this? Social anthropology. And fortunately, the methods of social anthropology are simple. They were in use two millennia ago.

In Luke ch.2 v 41 and following, we see the 12-year-old Jesus escape from his parents. While his mother and father are frantically searching for him, Jesus is hard at work putting anthropological methods into practice. Where is he? In the place where the Jewish leaders were: the very hub of Judaism. He would have been familiar with the milieu in provincial Nazareth or Cana, where he was growing up, but here in Jerusalem there was something different; not the semi-rural fishing and agricultural society that he was used to, but the society of the intelligentsia, the religious and political elite, in the very temple of God! He had already mastered the methods; now he was busy learning about the people he would later be working amongst and trying to reach.

And what are the methods? The first thing Jesus does is to *go there.* The brief visit he has made for the feast is not enough. He needs to be there for longer. He needs to be free to follow his own agenda: to get on with his father's work.

And what is he doing? *Listening* and *asking questions.*

To what can we attribute Jesus' acute knowledge and understanding of these people? It is clear, especially from John's Gospel, that later in his life he spoke to and treated the Pharisees and the teachers of the law quite differently from the 'multitudes.' Why was this? When, at the healing of the paralytic in his own village (and very probably in his own home), he knew what the Pharisees and teachers of the law were thinking, was it just spiritual intuition and perception, or was it also the deep knowledge that comes from observing, questioning and listening to the people who were essentially different from his own immediate society? Jesus was able to understand the Pharisees, their culture and their way of thinking, because he had been there; he had taken time to ask questions and to listen.

Furthermore, Jesus never gave up the habit of just *watching*. In the middle of a busy day he sits down to watch people putting money in the Temple offering box.(Mark ch.12 v.41), and is focused enough to see, among the great and the good giving their largesse, the widow giving her two tiny coins. He is even observing closely enough to see what they are worth.

These methods are so simple that they can be summarised on the back of an envelope:

- Find a context, and be there
- Make sincere relationships
- Show genuine love
- Watch
- Ask questions about what you see and hear
- Listen
- Ask more questions
- Learn!

We can either use this framework as a secular anthropologist might, where we are concerned only about our own work and care little about giving something back, or we can be motivated by love and respect for our neighbour, and by our desire to enjoy a genuine relationship with them and to see them rescued as part of God's plan.

Be there

First you need to be in a place or situation where you can get to know people in a very normal way. Jesus went right to the centre of Jewish faith, power and influence: the temple. He immediately involved himself in the business of the day, studying, teaching and debating theology. Christians have a tradition of working in medicine, teaching and other vocational jobs, and these are very useful, but there are endless other opportunities we can find: working in a post office or shop, as a receptionist, a mechanic in a garage, a cleaner, or a painter and decorator. A close friend of mine spent many hours repairing his old white van in the street, and in the prevailing car culture this was a great way of getting to know the other young men in the area. Lying with head under the van, feet sticking out all over the pavement and covered in oil was an open invitation to chat and work together.

Working in pairs or groups is also far better than working as an individual. A walk round the area where

Muslim people live in your town will bring up endless possibilities to a receptive imagination.

You may be looking at a serious time commitment where a part or full time job would be appropriate. Otherwise there is plenty of voluntary work where you can tailor the time to suit yourself. Muslim women often find it hard to leave their homes, but it is very easy for non-Muslim women to get *into* Muslim homes. A delightful feature of Islamic cultures is 'the visit', which is exactly what it sounds like: people go into each other's homes, just to visit. There is no agenda. In Western culture we need a reason or an invitation, but to visit your Muslim friend's home you need neither and you will be welcomed and appreciated. A Muslim woman may have difficulty going out anywhere other than to close relatives and friends, but may welcome regular visits from a non-Muslim female friend to learn English. Teaching English may lead to maturing relationships, and is liberating and empowering to the lady who is learning. I have spoken to dozens of women of all ages who would deeply appreciate this.

Sport too is a wonderful door-opener. Many Asian kids are deadly serious about cricket, and your football can be the most important item of equipment you have, after your Bible. All these activities will lead naturally into forming relationships. A friend who had no particular calling to work with Muslim people now has an ongoing dialogue with a number of Pakistani taxi drivers, and is reading the Bible with one of them.

In the 1980s my wife and I worked in an NHS general practice where more than 90% of the clientele were Muslim people from a Pakistani background. They knew it was a 'Christian place', but felt very at ease going there; in fact the numbers of Muslim people attending the practice increased by leaps and bounds, doubling in three years. Many said that our Christian basis was what attracted them.

The surgery turned out to be an ideal situation for making relationships, for sharing God's love, and for learning about our Muslim friends. When you drag yourself out of bed at 3am to visit a sick child, there is not too much pretence on either side. We got to know people well that way, and they got to know us. The practice also had the great advantage of being a team rather than an individual venture, and of being closely linked to the church where some of us worshipped. We were flexible in that where one person might find that they could not get on with a particular individual, another found them perfectly congenial. Many of our

Muslim friends felt that they had a relationship with the team rather than with one person.

This arrangement was perfect for us, but there are countless other opportunities awaiting people with imagination. What is crucial is that whatever the context, it should be entered into with honour and commitment. Jesus did not just talk, he worked. He went about doing good, and he made a good job of it. Our presence should involve a worthy task in itself, and not just be treated as a platform for achieving another agenda.

Make sincere relationships

Why are we forming relationships? Because God first sent his only son so that we could have a relationship with him. Relationships take time, maybe months or years. Often the growth of a relationship is less dependent on the number of encounters you have had than how much time has passed; people I have met only two or three times in a couple of years feel that we know each other. With my terrible memory I am constantly embarrassed when I bump into someone who I have met once or twice over three years and who feels on that account that they know me well.

Your relationship exists firstly for itself and for the other person; and here we part company from the professional anthropologist. Your friend is your friend; your friendship has no ulterior purpose. Your friends must never become just 'useful', and we include here your desire to share the Good News. When the time comes that, as your friend, you have a deep desire to share what is most precious to you, then the moment has come for you to look for an opening. But perhaps your friend will ask you first! Our relationships must be entirely free from hidden agendas. We achieve this by simply being honest about who we are and what we are interested in.

Show genuine love

St Francis is said to have said, "Preach the Gospel constantly; if necessary use words". For us, the point is this: the Good News is Good News about God's love, and our words will rightly fall on deaf ears if they do not come from a life of love. The trouble we encounter with this is that love is nearly always time-consuming, very likely to cost money as well as time, often boring, personally very taxing and seriously exhausting. One morning after a long and difficult surgery I lay on the floor of the consulting room in a state of complete exhaustion. I knew at that moment exactly what a dishcloth feels like when the washing-up is finished. We found that the work of a GP's surgery gave us all endless opportunities to show love, often to the unlovely and the feckless, at times when we should have gone home hours ago. Often it meant doing a home visit when that was not really necessary, and often it meant listening on and on, and in so doing keeping others waiting. Often it just meant being kind and gentle to those who never experience any kindness or gentleness. I have seen nurses and doctors behave with the most shocking unkindness and rudeness in several countries, and many of our Pakistani clientele told us of similar experiences 'at home'. To treat the sick and old with consideration, politeness and gentleness has an amazing impact - though we don't do it for impact, we do it because this is simply the right way. This is the way Jesus treated people, and this is the way he treats us. "Love one another as I have loved you". This is not only the best motivation for our behaviour; it is the only one. It sustains you long after the warm feel-good factor has gone and you are screaming with tiredness or confusion.

Watching and listening

We have some understanding of what people are doing in our own culture. When we are within someone else's culture, we are conscious that often we have no idea of what is going on. Furthermore, there may be pictures, symbols and other items whose meaning we take for granted, but which in reality mean something quite different, and activities which we take to be about one thing but which in reality have a totally different significance. Why do people read the Qur'an for hours when someone dies? What is that writing over the front door? What is that thing your baby has round its neck? Familiarity can lead us to ignore these things, but we need to observe them closely and ask ourselves what they are for. These are things that lead us to the 'gut' level, where the real beliefs that govern people's behaviour and give meaning to their lives are to be found. More difficult are things that are so normal for us that we fail to ask whether they signify something entirely different in the other culture. This family has lots of money so why do the little girls always look dirty? How good it is that to listen and observe with love is not only the way to learn, it is also the right and respectful way to treat people who will nearly always respond to your interest.

Ask questions

In the late 1990s, after I had been working as a family doctor for six years, I started on a research degree, the subject of which was what Muslim men and women actually believe and do, rather than what the theological textbooks say they should be doing and believing. At the outset this required me to spend many hours asking questions of the people I had got to know well in our surgery. I viewed this task with some anxiety; what would people think of me prying into their lives? Was I going to offend my friends to the point of alienating them? Would I have to show a great deal of the tact that I don't actually possess?

The task I had set myself initially was to find out about the tiny little black boxes that so many of the Muslim kids had hung round their necks on bits of string. I knew that they were related to folk beliefs that so many people held to, and I knew they were important. I actually made a detailed questionnaire that would help me find the information I was looking for, and to get started I had picked a family who I felt would not be too averse to my prying curiosity. With great tact I asked Jameela why her little baby had one of these little black boxes round her neck, and what it was for.

I hardly managed to get a word in edgeways for the next half an hour or so. Jameela simply couldn't stop talking.

"Oh yes, my grandma put it on her when we were in Pakistan, she said she needed it for protection. Its for the 'eye'."

"Do you think it works?"

Jameela laughed, "I'm not sure really. I mean, I still take Fairouza to the surgery when she's ill."

"What would happen if you took it off her?"

"I'm scared to. I think I'll leave it on."

The questionnaire did not survive the first day. I had made the vital discovery that people like Jameela appreciate it so much when you are interested enough to ask questions about their lives, and love to talk freely about themselves. I am sure that I didn't actually get the answer that I was looking for, but what I did get was a fascinating and detailed insight into many aspects of Jameela's life and the way that she and her family thought. And I also got the answer to a lot of other questions.

We had moved a long way from the 'head' aspect of Islam, and were at the 'gut' level. Instead of a difficult talk about what Fatima believed about Islam, where she might quite possibly have felt that she needed to put on a show of being a good Muslim, we had begun to talk about the deep beliefs that actually motivated her life, and had touched on the powerfully influential occult beliefs that are below the surface in so many British Muslims, and which were represented by the talisman, the 'taweez', that Fairouza, her little girl, wore round her neck to protect her from the 'evil eye'.

As time went on, my experience was repeated countless times. Those whom I had known as patients in the surgery I came to know in a new way. I began to regret that I had not learned to ask questions much sooner, and was mortified to realise how little I actually knew about their lives. I slowly began to piece together a picture of what people's gut beliefs were. Every time I formed a tentative theory in my mind as to what was going on it was blown out of the window by the next person I spoke to. The talismans, the little tiny boxes wrapped in black cloth and hung round the neck with string, and which Jameela and others called taweez, have a bewildering number of origins and uses. As well as protection from the 'evil eye', teenagers used them because they believed that they would help them to pass their GCSE's. Two girls wanted them so they could watch horror videos late at night and not have bad dreams afterwards. Mothers used them to prevent their daughters falling in love with someone 'unsuitable'.

Many men did not believe in them but wore them 'just in case...'

Listening

For months I persisted with my questioning on this and many other matters, some of which are mentioned in the next chapter. No one ever seemed to get fed up with me, and I listened for hours to men and women, old and young, talking to me about themselves and their life experiences; djinns, angels, marriage, the universe and how to survive in it, sex and how to survive that, the Prophet and how to enlist his help and the help of his family, the Qur'an and how to access its blessings, how to ward off evil and enlist the good onto your side. Illness: where it comes from and how to deal with it, blessings and disasters, the evil eye - who carries it, its diagnosis and cure.

What to these people were the most mundane of matters was to me a revelation. I began to dimly understand both how alike we were and how different. We had truly arrived at the 'gut', the engine room, the place where the beliefs lie that shape the way that people live and function, the place they make sense of the world, and perhaps try to exert control over what goes on in it. We had left formal Islam, the Islam of the head, far behind - yet it was very much present. People regarded themselves as 'good Muslims', never for a moment considering that their folk beliefs and occult involvement were anything less than seamlessly compatible with formal theological Islam.

The more you ask questions, and the more you listen, the harder it will be to generalise about what you hear and what you discover. Nevertheless, you will gain a general feeling for what is going on. More importantly, you will learn much more about the very tiny group of individuals who you are in touch with. You will be gaining understanding, and perhaps love, for them.

Although there are some books that are helpful, no book can open the door that can be opened by sincere enquiry in the context of loving relationships. As I have said, we are not talking about 'people' in general, about Muslims *en bloc*, but about the people we know - the people we work with and who are our friends. They are the only ones who matter. After a while we will be able to draw out some generalisations, but we are not really trying to generalise, we are particularising our knowledge with a tiny number of people - we are finding out what these beliefs mean to our friends, their families, their street. We are forgetting the vast numbers of people 'out there', who we are not actually concerned with.

It is so easy to assume that magic is not something found in our own culture or even in our own faith, yet an anthropologist once said[1] that every doctor is uncomfortably aware that much medical practice is only a step away from magic. We are all rather conscious that we are giving someone a pill or an X-ray or some other treatment not because we are sure of the scientific benefit but because our patient feels that it will 'do them good.' Baptism, ("I want my child done, vicar") still has strong magic connotations in many parts of England that have nothing to do with its real purpose. The shrines and relics of medieval Christianity, and of Catholicism in South America, bear a striking resemblance to the practices of many Muslims today. If a Christian believes that when he or she takes Holy Communion the bread and wine have some effect in themselves, this is a magic belief in exactly the same way.

Conclusion

Jesus knew the hearts of the scribes and Pharisees. This enabled him to speak the truth about himself directly to them in a language they could understand. That does

[1] B. Malinowski; *Magic, Science and Religion, and Other Essays*, (Souvenir Press, 1948), p.88ff

not mean that they could accept what he said, but their rejection was not based on misunderstanding. It frequently happens that we speak the truth to Muslim people and they reject what we have to say because we use a language they do not understand. We will look at this in Chapter 6. But much of the rest of this book is about finding a common language.

And find it we must. We must communicate the good news to those who are ready and willing to hear it, and, occasionally, to those who are not. We must be ready, in St Paul's words, to "give an account of what we believe." As we are hauled into the lifeboat we turn to give a hand to the person in the water behind us. As we go into the feast we repeat the invitation to hungry people. The relationships we foster, and the treatment we offer to others, will open the door to speaking the truth of Christ as well as living it. When those opportunities occur we must grab them with both hands.

Chapter 3

God, etc.

We have moved from the head, passing through the heart, to the gut. We have seen that watching, asking questions and listening is the way to discover the secrets about the gut beliefs, not only of Muslim people, but of everyone. We have moved from the perspective of the theologian to that of the anthropologist. We are doing this because we love the people we are with and want to know them well; loving them as they are, not as we imagine them to be. We are doing this because we appreciate that Islam is not just 'religion' but an all-encompassing biosphere, of which culture and family, belief, politics, language and worldview are a part. We are doing this so that we can share the love of Christ with them at a deep level in a language they and we can understand.

To help us in our quest I offer some 'coat hangers'. These short notes are here not so much to provide information, but as guides for questioning and exploration. They also represent my personal viewpoint, and are derived largely from my own experience. They may be irrelevant or even untrue for the people who you are with, and you may find whole areas that I have missed out.

I am including here what many would regard as 'Islamic doctrine', but I have looked at these from an anthropological perspective rather than a theological one.

Allah

God is out there somewhere, very powerful, very remote. Because we all use the word 'God', we can easily fall into the trap of thinking that we are all talking about the same one. Here we encounter a language problem which we will tackle in more detail later. Enough to say that there are three 'gods' here - firstly Almighty God, as he actually is; secondly your own imperfect grasp of the God of the Bible as you yourself are striving to understand and love; and thirdly the concept of God in the head, heart and gut of your Muslim friend. It is the most natural thing for you to ask him or her what they think about God, who they believe he is, what he is like, and how they think God views them. You may get a ready answer from the head, but often the answer from the gut is not so quickly forthcoming. A young drug addict, was terrified of following Christ as he felt that 'Allah' would come after him and inflict a dreadful revenge. This fear came from the gut and had a much deeper effect than his well-established head knowledge of the God of Islam.

In Islam, God says much but actually does little. Furthermore he is entirely unpredictable, being free to act in any way he chooses at any time. The idea of 'covenant', where God, being all powerful, nevertheless decides by his own choosing to behave towards us in a certain consistent way, is alien to Islam.

The Oneness of God, the Idea of God's mathematical unity, is immensely important. This is *tawheed.* To associate anything or anyone with God in any way is to compromise the unity of God. This is called the 'sin of association', or *shirk.* God is extremely jealous of his oneness, and this is the greatest sin a Muslim can commit.

Kierkegaard called this 'The central idolatry of Islam'. If we can get our heads round this a great deal will fall into place. The oneness of God is like a great totem pole that runs from the head, through the heart, to the gut. It is certainly the biggest stumbling block to Muslims and darkens any discussion of the relationship between God the Father and his son Jesus.

"God is one" is overridingly the most important characteristic of the God of Islam; far more so than the God of the Bible, who is indeed one, but whose oneness is not unduly emphasised. More prominent are the unique features of God's character; his holiness and righteousness, his 'slowness to anger', his steadfast love and faithfulness, his dire hatred of sin and his willingness to forgive. God's oneness in Islam is an end in itself and is his most precious characteristic; it also, very specifically and categorically, precludes him from having a son.

Furthermore, in Islam God's oneness is of a different kind. God's oneness in the Old Testament is in contrast to the other false deities encountered by his people, the Baals and other 'gods' of the surrounding tribes that his people are commanded to turn their backs on: "You shall have no other gods beside me," (Deut. ch.5 v.7). The Israelites are enjoined to love God in the very same breath that God's Oneness is classically stated. "Hear O Israel, the LORD our God, the LORD is one. Love the LORD your God with all your heart, and with all your soul and with all your strength," (Deut. ch.6 v.4). When Moses asks God how he is to identify him to his people God says to Moses, "I AM who I AM." Who God is and what he is like is much more important than the fact that he is one.

The word for 'one' here is the same word that the writer of Genesis uses for the coming together of man and woman in marriage: "They shall become one flesh," (Genesis ch.2 v.18-25). The man and the woman in marriage are undoubtedly two persons, yet they are called 'one' with the same word that is used to tell us of the oneness of God. It is obvious that a simple and rigorous mathematical singularity is not what is being described here, but a complex relational and physical coming together of differences to make a whole. This prefigures the Trinity, the complex difficulty of which Christians often apologise for but which is a delightfully simple truth.

It is notable that 'oneness' is a mathematical quality, not a moral one. I had a long email discussion with Saleem, an Ahmadiyya leader on this topic. He was sure that oneness was self-evidently a moral quality. I was not. We failed to convince each other!

Much is made of the illiteracy and lack of formal education of the Prophet Muhammad. However, there is no doubt that he was a businessman and an accountant, and would have been well used to thinking mathematically. He also had no surviving son. It is worth considering what influence these facts may have had on his view of the oneness of Allah, and the very serious evil of ascribing a son to him.

After his oneness, the idea of God's sovereignty and judgement is immensely strong In Islam; and his goodness, holiness, love and compassion much less so. There is very little concept of love or intimacy or 'relationship' between God, his Prophet and his people. The cause of this is easily seen; the unity and oneness of God is very rigid, at the cost of the personal and the relational.

For the great majority of people (but not for all), God does not relate in a way that Christians understand, and this is the reason why Muslims will often say the things they do about Christianity. Why do Muslim people find it so hard to grasp the concept of the Trinity, and reject it comprehensively? Because there is no idea of relationship in connection with God, there is only isolated Unity.

The whole concept of God's rescue plan is incomprehensible to those who have not been introduced to the extraordinary idea of God's love. Without love the whole thing is ridiculous, and explains why so many of my Muslim friends will look on God's plan of salvation as 'too easy'.

Nevertheless, many Muslims in Britain are Sufis, who do not accept the Sunni attitude of the rigorous separation of God and his aloofness from men and women. There are also many people who, deep down, cannot countenance a world where God cares nothing about them. There is a gulf that is filled in a variety of ways, such as magic, or devotion to the Prophet.

Your Muslim friend may point you in the direction of the 'Beautiful Names', the 99 names of God. You can easily find a list of these names online. [2]

Many of these connect immediately with the God of the Old Testament, and it is obvious that without Yahweh, Allah could not exist. Yet there are some notable absences: nowhere among the beautiful names is the name 'Saviour' or 'Rescuer' to be found, an idea that features strongly in the Old Testament, and is backed up by his behaviour towards his people.

[2] http://sufism.org/foundations/ninety-nine-names/the-most-beautiful-names-of-allah-2

When looking at the beautiful names, there are three further drawbacks when you come to discuss them with your Muslim friend.

The first is how your friend has experienced what the names actually mean. I spoke to Rafiq about the mercy of Allah, a quality that Muslims mention time and time again when they pray. "In the name of God, the Merciful, the compassionate."

"Rafiq, how have you personally experienced the mercy of God?" I ask.

Rafiq tells me that he hopes that in the future God will be merciful to him.

"But isn't Allah merciful *now*, today? Does that not mean that he will be merciful all the time because that is his character?"

"Not necessarily...God can act in any way he chooses at any time," says Rafiq. "He may be merciful and forgiving, He may not. That is up to God. He will treat me as he wills. In fact," Rafiq goes on, "because God is all the time entirely free to act as he wishes; even if I live a perfect life he is under no obligation to send me to Heaven. And the opposite is true as well: I can have lived a really terrible life, never prayed or anything, and have never done a single good thing, but God is free to send me to Paradise, It is entirely the will of Allah!"

The second drawback to understanding the beautiful names is linking God's character to his behaviour. As Christians we are familiar with the idea that God's character can be understood from his behaviour towards us. We do not only read that God is faithful, we understand something of his faithfulness to his people as the story of the Bible unfolds, and from his faithfulness to us during our lifetimes. This idea does not seem to be a rewarding line of discussion, and in fact is linked to the third drawback.

"Can I learn something of what God is like by the human meaning of the beautiful names? I asked Ashraf, an imam in the north of England. "I mean, is Allah 'merciful' in the same way as one person might be towards another, like a victorious general towards his enemies, or a judge be towards a convicted criminal, something like that?"

"Oh no!" replied Ashraf. "That would be to say that God is like us human beings, and he is not! God is not like us!"

So we came to the conclusion that we don't really know what 'merciful' means. Ashraf went on to explain that the mercy of human beings is not at all the same as the mercy of God; if it was, we could say that we would truly know the character of God, and that is impossible.

It appears then, that the beautiful names don't tell us as much about Allah as we might have hoped. In fact, they are more useful as an aid to devotion.

Mansoor is very elderly and devout. He has the orange-dyed beard of one who has recently been on the pilgrimage. I ask him about the beads that he is holding. He holds his string of beads and gently moves from one to the next as he murmurs something under his breath. He explains that each bead is one of the beautiful names of Allah. He goes through them one by one.

I have had discussions about how God can be both merciful and just at the same time. Abu Bakr is from the Caribbean and owns an Islamic bookshop. He cannot see the problem. God does not need to be all of his attributes at once; he may be merciful today and just tomorrow. It is up to God. God will do what he wants at any time.

God's capriciousness is perhaps one of the main reasons why Muslim people are so involved in magic. Here they can attempt to exert some control in a universe where God is remote, where they can never be sure what his will is or what he will do, and in which they may well feel insecure and powerless.

So is the God of Islam the same God as the Christian God, or a different God? There are endless arguments in both directions, and the subtext here is usually the need to avoid unnecessary stumbling blocks as we try to present the Good News to our Muslim friends. These efforts are often built on the assumption that the closer Islam is to Christianity, the easier it might be for someone to 'become a Christian'.

I feel this genuine desire to accommodate people is misplaced for two reasons. Firstly, as I have said, the Good News of Jesus makes no sense unless God is as he is portrayed in the Bible.

Secondly, the men and women I have personally encountered who have had a deep experience of God have all felt they needed to make a break with Islam and its God. Part of the Good News is that the commonly held view of Allah is not what God is actually like.

It is worth considering that Allah, the God of Islam, is a little bit like ourselves; definitely made in the image of God, but fatally flawed and fatally inadequate. This is not an idea that is likely to commend itself in your conversations with your Muslim friend, but it might help a little in your own understanding.

The Prophet

Muslims, especially British Pakistani Muslims, are deeply devoted to the Prophet Muhammad. God is remote, but the Prophet is close at hand and very present in the consciousness of Muslims.

I asked Asif, a leading disciple of a very prominent 'pir' (a Sufi leader and spiritual guide) and a charismatic Muslim leader,

"Who do you love most in Islam?"

"Why, the Prophet of course!" He smiled.

What do Muslim people *really* believe? Part of the answer is that they believe deeply in the Prophet, love him passionately and will defend his honour fiercely. *The Satanic Verses*, by Salman Rushdie (who is himself a Muslim), is a fictional account of parts of the Prophet's life that were in part highly unflattering and cast doubts on the Prophet's veracity. Its publication and aftermath in the 1980s came as huge surprise both to Muslims and secular British people. To Muslims, because they never dreamt that someone could insult their Prophet so flagrantly in public and get away with it. To secular

British people, because their assumptions about robust knock-about free speech were comprehensively rejected in the subsequent furore. Many Muslim people rioted and publicly burned copies of the book to demonstrate their horror. At stake was the honour of the Prophet. Young people were bussed in to bolster the crowds of demonstrators. I spoke to teenagers at the time. They regarded the whole affair as great entertainment and an opportunity to party.

More recently, cartoons featuring Muhammad have been published which have aroused fury amongst Muslims, who have leapt to the defence of their Prophet, and aroused a corresponding anxiety in non-Muslims. As with *The Satanic Verses* the matter is complicated, and racked up emotionally by the need to be seen defending the Prophet's honour.

There are relics of the Prophet in Britain that are held in great reverence. At a birthday celebration of the Prophet I was taken to see a hair of the Prophet's head which, I was told, has continued to grow ever since his death many hundreds of years ago. Like the Prophet himself - who, I was assured, cast no shadow while he was alive - it has no shadow. This hair is in a gold casket and there are powerful lights to emphasise its translucency. Relics of the Prophet such as this are held to have great healing properties.

The birthday of the Prophet is a time of great feasting and rejoicing. I was fortunate enough to be invited to the birthday celebrations at one of Britain's largest and most prestigious mosques. Here many hundreds of men and women are entertained at great cost. There is much speechmaking and preaching; many mementos of the Prophet and CDs of songs in his praise are on sale together with books and pamphlets extolling his peerless character and unparalleled wisdom. Helium balloons adorned with Qur'anic texts are released in to the air; there is a noisy and colourful procession through the surrounding streets, carefully arranged to pass by as many churches as possible.[3] We are here at the heart level, and the deeply emotional nature of Islamic belief is here for all to see.

The Islamic view of the Prophet is to a great extent non-historical, and Muslim bookshops are full of pamphlets that tell of his life and virtues with no attempt to provide historical evidence. I have read booklets that

[3] Robin Fisher; "Change and Stability in an Urban Muslim Society", ch.2, 'Piri Maridi' (M.Phil thesis, University of Birmingham, 1997)

extol the virtues of Muhammad as husband, father, mediator, lawgiver, peacemaker, statesman, war leader...the list is endless. Even miracle worker, thought the Qur'an expressly tells us that Muhammad did no miracles. Many Muslim people have a strongly Messianic view of the Prophet, and believe in his pre-existence before his life on earth.

In spite of all this, it is true to say that perhaps for the first time in history there is overt criticism of the Prophet within Islam. An old man in a coffee shop in eastern Sudan starts shouting. "We have been Muslims for 200 years! What has the Prophet and Islam done for us? Let's get rid of them! Let's try Christianity!"

People are quick to agree, and others are quick to jump to the defence of the Prophet, but what is not questioned is that this subject is open for discussion. The taboo against any adverse comment about the Prophet Muhammad seems, for the moment, to have been forgotten.

The Qur'an

Along with deep love for and belief in the Prophet comes a profound reverence for the Qur'an, as the revelation from God that he brought. With the Prophet, and the 'one-ness' of God, it is the most deeply embedded belief in the heart and gut of most Muslims. It is regarded as 'the Word of God', and believed to have been dictated verbatim to the Prophet. It is not really possible to be a Muslim and have a less categorical belief than this. I said to Karim, a middle-aged Sudanese man, "have you ever once thought the unthinkable? Have you ever considered that the Qur'an might in some places be mistaken?"

"If I ever, even for an instant thought that" he replied, "I would have ceased to be a Muslim."

Nevertheless, some Muslims in the West are beginning to think the unthinkable.

Both the Qur'an and the Bible are paper between two covers, but that is where the similarity ends. For Christians, the Bible is not God's last word to men and women. That place is held by Jesus; whereas for Muslims, the Qur'an is God's last and best word to mankind.

Beyond this, most Muslims view the Qur'an in an entirely different way than Christians view their scriptures. The Christian idea is that it is the content that matters, that it reveals the true character of God and his work, that it is to be studied and enjoyed, 'read, marked, learned and inwardly digested', and that reading it leads to growth and maturity as a Christian. Not only that, but that it is definitely not a 'magic book', and can be held to account historically and critically. It can be and has been subject to the most rigorous analysis and criticism.

These ideas are entirely absent from the minds of most Muslim people, who regard any questioning or criticism of the Qur'an as anathema. Total and unquestioning acceptance is usually seen as a sign of deep piety. This idea is of course closely linked to the Islamic philosophy of education, as we shall see, and displays a feature of pre-Enlightenment thinking which involves the acceptance of authority - the opinions of scholars and imams - without questioning or holding them to account.

A huge majority of Muslims in Britain and worldwide do not speak or read Arabic, the language of the Qur'an, which has been translated into only a dozen or so languages. This in itself tells us something about the meaning, i.e. that it is not of prime importance. It has been said that 'the fact that the Qur'an exists is more important than what it says.'[4]

In fact many Muslims who do not speak Arabic can recite huge portions of the Qur'an by heart and know almost nothing of what it means. This is because the meaning itself is secondary; the taking of the Qur'anic words themselves, independently from the meaning, into the mind brings 'baraka' - or blessing and benefit.

I visited Hamid, a young drug addict in prison. He told me that he was a 'Hafiz', a 'keeper' of the Qur'an, because he had learned it by heart from start to finish and was able to recite it aloud word perfect. He had been at a special ceremony and had a green bandanna and shawl awarded to him to prove it. Hamid is from a Pakistani background and knows no Arabic. I asked him what good it had done him. "Well Doc," he said with a laugh, "So far, not a lot!"

Khadija is a middle-aged lady. If you have a problem you can go to her and she will write some words from the Qur'an on a slip of paper in water-soluble ink. She will instruct you to go home and immerse the paper in a

---

[4] Andrew Rippin; *Muslims: Their Religious Beliefs and Practices, vol.ii, The Contemporary Period* (Routledge, 1993)

glass of water. When the ink has completely disappeared off the paper you are to drink the water. The dissolved words have gone into your body and you will receive baraka. The word means 'blessing', but the concept is without the moral overtones that we associate with it. Fatima's little girl, Aisha, wears a talisman round her neck. In it is a tiny piece of paper; on it are written some verses of the Qur'an. If Aisha continues to wear this taweez she will receive baraka in the form of protection from the 'evil eye'. Basima, a teenage girl, would like to be able to watch violent DVDs without having subsequent nightmares, and her friend is desperate to get good marks in her GCSEs. Both have taweez with Qur'anic verses inscribed on them, and believe that this will get them what they wish.

Baraka also comes from hearing the Qur'an read, or rather intoned, aloud; the technique requires much practice and training and a good exponent is admired and sought after. To hear the Qur'an sung in this way can be deeply moving for worshippers. Sleeping on the roof of our flat in eastern Sudan I would wake in the early hours in the unaccustomed silence, when the dozen or so electricity generators within ear shot had been closed down, the cassette-radios had been switched off, and the packs of wild dogs had finally fallen asleep. Trying hard to stay awake so that I could enjoy the silence, I would wait for the early morning call to prayer from the mosque nearby to shatter the peace. Allaaaaahu Akhbar..Allahu akhbar, God is great! Once over, the call to prayer would be followed by the early morning Qur'anic recitation, long, drawn-out sentences in high pitched sing-song Arabic cadences displaying amazing breath control. It is a highly developed art form, with its own beauty. In between verses there would be deep, heartfelt groans of "Allahu Akhbar", and gasps of ecstasy from the worshippers. This was more, to them, than just a reading from scripture.

Arabic

The language of the Qur'an is in indispensible part of its mystique. Arabic is a wonderfully expressive language, full of poetry and high-sounding cadences. It has a complicated grammar that is not used in everyday speech but is reserved for formal and religious use. This is mirrored in the script, where the vowel and other grammatical signs are not written, except in religious writings and sacred texts, such as the Qur'an. Furthermore, Arabic writing has been raised to a fine art. Stimulated by the injunction against visual images, huge amounts of talent and effort have been devoted to calligraphy. Arabs and non-Arabs alike can appreciate the beauty of decorated inscriptions and the ornamented writing of the Qur'an itself. Muslims will tell you that the Qur'an cannot be translated out of the original Arabic. As the language itself is so much part of the message, this is no doubt true. The mystery and drama is hugely amplified in the many Muslim ears that do not understand the Arabic language and hence have only a second-hand idea of the meaning.

There is no clearer example of 'head, heart and gut' than with the significance of the Qur'an. The deep indoctrination and acceptance of its authority in the head, the poetry of the language and the music of Qur'anic chanting in the heart, and its use in magic and the occult in the gut.

Not all Muslims believe that the Qur'an acts in this magical way; I have heard one or two friends denounce the magical use of the Qur'an as 'complete rubbish'. It is good to find out from your Muslim friend how he or she views the Qur'an, how they or their family use taweez, and what for. You will certainly get some interesting answers. Increasingly, young Muslims are looking into the Qur'an to see what it actually says. If this happens, there may be some startling results as Muslims see that their holy book says things about Jesus that place him in a unique position, in a category of his own. We will look at this again in Chapter 13.

The Hajj

When you visit an Islamic bookshop, take a look at a picture that you may have seen many times, or seen on line if you Google 'Kaaba'. You might also have seen it in the homes of your friends. Firms put it on their annual gift calendars, and my local barber's shop has it. It is universal.

The picture is of the Kaaba, the central object within the Haraam Mosque, the greatest mosque in Mecca. It is at the climax of the Hajj, the pilgrimage on which every Muslim man and woman must go during his or her lifetime, to the holy city of Islam, where no unbeliever may tread. There are worshippers in their hundreds, covering every inch of ground and on every building, circling the Kaaba; all in white, all kneeling, all bowing with forehead to the ground in worship.

When your friend returns from the Hajj, ask them about what they felt and experienced. Some come away having had a deep spiritual experience. Often there is a huge sense of solidarity and oneness, of being part of the Umma, the global Muslim community. Some people are intoxicated; some bored. Some are terrified of being crushed to death in the crowd. Here is the heart of Islam, and for many it is a deeply emotional moment.

Although everyone is expected to go at least once in their lifetime, the honour of having been on the pilgrimage is great. Men dye their beards red, and women their hair when they have been on the Hajj. One way of respectfully addressing an elderly person is 'Hajji' for a man, and 'Hajja' for a lady.

The Umma

The pilgrimage is a powerful statement of the solidarity of Islam. Here is the Umma, the family of Islam; the 'Dar al Islam', (the House of Islam). The feeling of Umma is so great that it eclipses nationalistic feeling. In fact patriotic feeling for one's native country is very weak in most Muslim countries. Nearly all of such countries are young; some countries such as Bangladesh and Pakistan are actually younger than many of their citizens. National boundaries in the Middle East were unilaterally laid down by Western powers with no regard to the ethnicity or religious groupings of those living there, and this has much to do with the upheavals that are tearing the Middle East apart at the present time.

Religious politics

In the communities in Britain that originate from Pakistan, every political and religious grouping is faithfully replicated. The Naqshbandis, Deobandis

Barelvis and others, as well as their offshoots. There are also the Ahmadiyyas, who are regarded as beyond the pale by other Muslims, and who in the UK enjoy a freedom and security that would be unthinkable at home. This reproductive pattern is repeated in other immigrant communities, and is far from being unique to Islam, but it does indicate that there is, for the outsider, a bewildering complexity of religious politics. The good news is, as I said earlier, that we do not have to delve into all this; but we do have to know that it exists. Over and above all this is the divide between Sunnis, the largest grouping in Islam, who follow the practice of the Prophet, (the Sunna) and Shia's, the second largest, who consider Ali, son-in-law of the Prophet, to have been his successor, and who have many traditions and practices that differ from Sunnis. Many Shia Muslims in UK are Sufis, who belong to different orders, called tariqas, and much of the content of this chapter comes from Sufi sources. A feature of Sufism is that there are men of religious stature called pirs, who are mostly associated with shrines where previous pirs with miraculous powers have been buried. For instance, the Golden Hillock mosque in Small Heath, Birmingham, has as its parent the Ghamkol Mosque in Pakistan, and is under its very real and close supervision. Pirs are reckoned to have spiritual power, and many people have recourse to them. In modern day terminology, Sufis represent 'spiritual' Islam, the Islam of the heart. In many communities of Pakistani heritage, if it is not convenient or possible to make the pilgrimage, one might ask a pir or some other deeply respected person to do it for you. Many people have made the pilgrimage by proxy in this way, and one pir has made the pilgrimage more than two dozen times.

We need to listen to our Muslim friend as he or she tells us about the particular grouping that they belong to, why it is the correct and perfect way, and why the others are in error, or worse, 'not Islam'. I have heard Muslim academics in universities writing off the people in other parts of the town. A visiting lecturer, commenting on the practices of other communities in the town tells me, "These are uneducated village people; this is not Islam - don't listen to them!" My reply to this kind of remark is invariably that I, a non-Muslim, cannot possibly presume to tell what is Islam and what is not. These are my friends, and as far as I can see their beliefs and yours are all Islam because they tell me so, and I accept that.

We need to listen, but it is important for us not to be sidetracked. Our aim is to get to the heart, and a discussion of religion and its minutiae will never take us there. We need to listen, and hear, but we need to develop ways of moving from the religious to the personal.

Chapter 4

Fear

Abdu leaned over the balcony of a Cairo flat, blowing smoke rings.

"All Islamic governments operate through fear," he said.

A dissident Sudanese politician, who had done time in prison, Abdu was an asylum seeker. He knew what he was talking about.

"All Islam operates through fear," he added, after a moment's reflection.

Fear and violence are deeply rooted within Islam. There is also a degree of fear of Islam in the wider community, and in Britain this very much includes other minority ethnic groups as well. I recall a number of conversations with Indian Hindu men who expressed anxiety at the power of the Muslim community and their perceived greater political influence.

However, my main concern is to point up the fear which is within Islam, and which helps maintain high barriers to the outside world and control within.

All four schools of Sharia law call for the death penalty for men who forsake Islam, and lesser (but severe) penalties for women. This runs directly against the UN declaration on human rights but nevertheless, it is law in many Muslim countries where Sharia law forms the basis of statute law. Sharia law has no force in the UK but is a powerful statement of the way Islam views those who leave it. It would be hard or impossible to find any organisation in the UK that maintains its barriers in this way.

Further afield, Christians, and those exploring and investigating the Christian faith from within Islam, are under intense pressure and persecution all over the Middle East. This is a sideshow to the way that Muslim groups, both political and religious, persecute each other and seem unable to solve difficulties or compromise without violence - a direct legacy of the birth of Islam and its Prophet.

This fear originates directly in the character of the Prophet, the Qur'an, and Islam's early history.

The warlike life of the Prophet

Ali Dashti, a Muslim Iranian theologian, gives an account of the Prophet Muhammad's life.[5] Initially peaceful, the Prophet became more warlike as he gained power;[6] the young Muslim community was maintained to a large extent by raids on camel trains in the desert. In his wars against the Jews the Prophet executed over 600 members of the Aws tribe that had surrendered to him. He also ordered a number of men to be assassinated.[7] The Prophet took part personally in a number of battles.[8] This would matter less if the life of the Prophet and his example were not constantly present to Muslims. Islamic history is of great importance to Muslim people, who tend to be much more aware of their history than Westerners.

The Qur'an

The shift from peaceful to warlike means in the Prophet's life is reflected in the Qur'an, which contains

---

[5] Ali Dashti; *Twenty-Three Years, a Study of the Prophetic Career of Mohammad* (Mazda Publishers, 1994)
[6] ibid, p.97
[7] ibid, p.98-99
[8] ibid

injunctions to fight unbelievers and enemies of Islam:[9]
"O, You who believe, fight the unbelievers who gird you
about and let them find firmness in you," (Sura 9 v.123).
"When the forbidden months are past, then find and slay
the pagans wherever you find them, and seize them and
beleaguer them and lie in wait for them in every
stratagem of war," says Sura 9 v.4, adding that if they
"repent and establish regular prayers the way may be
made open for them."

These are only two of a number of similar verses. Taking
of ransom for prisoners is also sanctioned (Sura 8 v.58).
Almost more important is what is not stated: nowhere
in the Qur'an is there any guidance on how to behave in
a cooperative way with non-Muslims or live at peace
with them. A state of conflict is invariably assumed. The
aggressive standpoint of the Qur'an is reinforced by the
Hadith - 'The Traditions' - which are almost as
influential.[10]

The Islamic community calls itself the Umma, 'the
Family'; or the 'Dar al Islam', the 'House of Islam'. There

---

[9] See also The Holy Qur'an, Sura 9 v.5, 12, 13, 14, 29, 36, 38,
41, 68, 73
[10] Bernard Lewis; *The Crisis of Islam*, ch.2, "The House of War",
p.27

is only one other 'house' and that is all people who are not Muslims, who are called the 'Dar al Harb' - the 'House of War'. Islam is historically set against non-Muslims, and the cultural boundaries between the two are very marked.

Jihad

The Prophet enjoins the believers to jihad, which means 'striving'. Coming from the same root as 'Mujahideen', meaning 'freedom fighter', jihad is one of the central tasks of the faithful Muslim. Many apologists insist that this is a peaceful spiritual struggle, and this may well be part of its meaning, but it is quite clear that there is a very strong military aspect. Again, in the Qur'an, we can see how the peaceful and 'spiritual' use of the term gives way to a more physical and aggressive tone in the later Suras, though both senses are connected. A good example is Sura 4 v.95:[11] "Not equal are those believers who sit at home and receive no hurt, and those who strive and fight in the cause of God with their goods and possessions God hath granted a grade higher to those who strive and fight with their goods and persons than those who sit at home."

[11] *The Holy Quran,* Text, Translation and Commentary by Abdullah Yusuf Ali

While the more peaceful aspects of jihad are emphasised by those who are keen to present Islam as peaceful, earlier commentators and Islamic Law as a whole tend to present jihad in strongly military terms. It is a religious obligation for the defence of Islam and the furtherance of Islamic power. Usama bin Ladin was inspired by the call to jihad - firstly in Afghanistan, and then elsewhere.[12]

Military campaigns

From the beginning, Islam was spread by the most brilliant and sustained military operation. Within a very short space of time, victorious Muslim armies all but destroyed the empire of Persia, overran much of Central Asia, and conquered and Islamicised Palestine, Syria, Egypt and the rest of North Africa. By the early eighth century much of Spain and Portugal had been conquered, and Muslim armies were crossing the Pyrenees. Only after many hundreds of years were the invaders rolled back. In various forms, offensive jihad

---

[12] Bernard Lewis; *The Crisis of Islam*, ch.2 "The House of War". Lewis gives a useful account of Jihad, and the effect it has on present day thinking, especially that of Usama Bin Ladin. Also Bill Musk; *Holy War*, ch.2 "The World's Most Wanted Man" discusses the influence of Jihad on Usama bin Ladin.

continued until the early nineteenth century.[13] While many Western people are hardly aware of this very significant history, Muslims by and large are highly conscious of the early years of their religion, and of what they see as shameful subservience to Western powers during and after the age of colonialism.

Laws of apostasy

As I mentioned earlier, the laws on apostasy which are derived from the Hadith[14] dictate that those who leave Islam for another religion should suffer death if a man, and imprisonment, divorce and loss of her children if a woman. In some countries such as Saudi Arabia, this penalty is likely to be carried out. In Britain it is not unknown for Christians from Islamic backgrounds to be quietly taken back to the countries where their families originate and killed. They may alternatively suffer threats and physical harm. While these dire penalties are carried out to the letter only infrequently, their continued presence in the Sharia in Western multicultural countries suggests that Muslim leaders may be too fearful of their constituents to make changes.

[13] Bernard Lewis, ibid.
[14] *Leaving Islam*, Ibn Warraq ed. (Prometheus Books, 2003), chs. 7-9.

Boundaries

Within Islamic communities there is a general looking-out-for those who are reckoned to be getting near cultural and religious boundaries; a girl making friends with a non-Muslim, or with any man not chosen for her by her father (in reality her mother, who has access to eligible young women), whether Muslim or not; any woman dressing in a way not reckoned to be acceptable in her social or family circle; anyone showing interest in Christianity or any other faith; or anyone becoming involved in a profession that is not seen as appropriate, such as nursing. These activities reflect on the honour of the man in the family, which is closely bound up with the behaviour of women under his roof. In many Muslim cultures a man's honour is upheld when his daughters marry the man chosen for her by her family, who is frequently a close relative.

This does not mean that all Muslim people are frightened all the time. This is patently not true. But it does mean that as a person moves towards the boundaries of their society they may experience coercion or threats. Nor does it mean that Muslims are more violent than other people - I have known very many Muslim people in many countries, and have no hesitation in affirming that the vast majority have been entirely peaceful, law-abiding citizens. What it does mean is that fervent Muslims looking for inspiration may well be guided to the warlike passages in the Qur'an. There can be no 'radicalisation' without this foundation and basis in the practice of the Prophet. It is at least possible to suggest that Muslim people remain peaceful at the expense of being 'good Muslims'. I am suggesting here that although Muslim people are by nature no more violent or warlike than anyone else, their religion contains justification for behaviour that is both violent and warlike.

Family

Many Muslims have told me that if it were not for fear and pressure from their family, they would be Christians; but the price is just too high. These people are not Muslims because they are convinced of the truth of Islam - they are Muslims through fear. A young man who had become a Christian two years previously was at our home when two men who would now be called 'fundamentalists' arrived for a discussion. Jamil initially sat silently during the conversation, but then quietly gave an account of how he had left Islam, and of his very clear experience of Christ. Since his conversion he had studied Islam critically, and in the ensuing discussion the two preachers were unable hold their ground, to their very obvious unease and annoyance.

As they left, thinking that they were out of earshot, they threatened Jamil with death. Two days later Jamil was attacked in the street near his home; he escaped with minor injuries and was whisked off into hiding to a farm in the country. For two years his father would not allow him into his home and he had to arrange secret visits with his mother. It is sad that after many years of courageously holding onto his Christian faith, the physical and emotional pressure became too great, and he has finally reverted to Islam. Has he become a Muslim because he is newly convinced of the truth of Islam? Of course not. He has overcome fear, but huge social and family pressure has drawn him back into the Islamic biosphere, back into the Dar al Islam.

Wakeel, a young economics undergraduate, visited us in our home in Jordan faithfully almost every week. As we consistently read the Bible together he grew as a Christian, but we could never get him to meet others of the same faith or to come to church with us. He was just too terrified of his family finding out that he had become a Christian. Maqbool was much older, in his 50s, and a successful manager of a shirt factory. He had come to know Christ during a long stay at a Christian hospital. At last we managed to persuade these two to meet. It was a truly wonderful day. For Wakeel it was the very first time that he had met a Muslim who had become a Christian.

"If my father knew that I was here he would kill me," he said.

"If my son knew that I was here he would kill me," replied Maqbool.

It is exceptionally difficult to arrange for Christians to meet together in some countries both because of the fear that their faith will be discovered, and the deep mutual suspicion that that is engendered in this situation.

Abd al Ali is a Bible translator; during his five years contract he was consumed with fear that his job would be discovered and he would be treated as a rebel and an apostate by his family. And he has not even become a Christian.

Abid was a 24 year-old drug addict. He had been in trouble with the police on countless occasions but had now successfully come off drugs and had made a firm commitment to follow Christ. He was starting the slow and painful process of learning to lead a more or less normal life. Abid described how his mother, sensing that there had been changes in his life and behaviour, pinned him up against the wall and interrogated him. "Go to prison if you must," she screamed, "Do anything, anything, just don't become a Christian." Terrified that he had indeed done what they dreaded most, his family kidnapped him, and it was several days before he was able to escape.

In all these cases it is the family that that is at the root of people's fears. In Muslim countries security police and government come a long way second, though they hold their own terrors. The real fear is engendered by the need for the family to maintain its honour in the public arena.

Although nearly universal, this response is not inevitable. Khalid, a middle aged Sufi, lived not far from our surgery. He and I enjoyed frequent Bible readings and prayer. He clearly delighted in Jesus but had made no formal break with Islam. His wife, who was far more traditional, seemed to have only a token objection. A younger man in the same street made a much more conventional commitment to Christ in a very Western way, and was tolerated well by his unusually broadminded family. But these are exceptions to the rule. Muslims who become interested in the Bible invariably expect trouble.

In Britain generally there is a degree of apprehension relating to Islam that is not felt about Hinduism or Sikhism or other faiths. Those attempting to make contact with Muslim neighbours or colleagues may also experience anxiety; they may feel that they will be excessively sensitive, or react strongly to any attempt to start a conversation about the Good News. They may on occasion fear physical violence, and indeed my wife and myself have been the subject of death threats. When we hear protestations that 'Islam is a peaceful religion', or that 'Islam is a religion of peace and harmony', we need to ask what the Sharia law says should happen to Muslims if they become Christians (or in fact adopt any other religion).

These threats are far from idle. In Sudan an imam, who was also an army officer and well known to us, became a Christian and found himself in prison. After due legal process, he found himself facing the death penalty. Bizarrely, the judge gave him a week's leave before his sentence was due to be carried out, saying he was 'not in the business of killing Christians'. Only a successful escape from the country saved his life.

We need to remind our Muslim friends of the persecution endured by many Christians in the home countries of their families. Even this sometimes seems insignificant compared with the oppression endured by Muslim minorities in their own countries. My Ahmadiyya[15] friends in the north of England say that they feel far safer in Britain than 'at home' in Pakistan where they have endured unremitting persecution.

Of course very few Muslims live their lives with this rigorously separatist attitude. Our common experience is that we live alongside our Muslim friends and neighbours in peace and harmony. In our surgery we never felt even for a moment that we were the Dar al Harb, the 'House of War'. Actually we experienced the opposite; we felt loved and respected. Only a tiny minority look on non-Muslims as enemies, which is what the name 'House of War' implies. Nevertheless, there are situations that will trigger the powerful solidarity of the 'House of Islam', however disunited it may be internally, such as when the Prophet is challenged or insulted, or when a Muslim country is invaded. When someone is seen to be in danger of

[15] The Ahmadiyya sect of Islam has unorthodox beliefs that render it deeply unpopular in Pakistan, where most of its adherents live.

leaving Islam, especially to become a Christian, then the family and community will mobilise to 'protect' the individual concerned, and will exert enormous pressure on them. That is why many who are interested In the Christian Gospel sometimes seem to become more 'religious', taking pains to pray five times a day or at any rate attend mosque on Friday and if they are women perhaps wearing more Islamic clothing, thus putting up a smoke screen behind which they can carry on their 'head work'.

Chapter 5

Cultural Coathangers

Magic, the occult, and worldview

Magic can be defined as 'ascribing power to objects or rituals where there is no material connection'. The use of taweez or talismans is a good example of this. They are expected to affect events, health or other matters in the way I have already outlined above, and the use of texts from the Qur'an as I have outlined it above is magical as well.[16]

Occult activity is an attempt to use supernatural forces, or human beings who are viewed as having

---

[16] For a full treatment of this subject please see Mary Douglas; *Natural Symbols* (London: Barrie and Rockliff, The Cresset Press,1970); and B. Malinowski; *Magic, Science and Religion, and other Essays* (Souvenir Press, 1948).
For a fuller treatment of Magic as it is present in British Muslim societies, see Robin Fisher; *Change and Stability in an Urban Muslim Community*, (M.Phil thesis, Birmingham University, 1997).

supernatural power, to influence people or events for good or for ill.

To many Muslims, there is nothing so mundane as magic. It is the simple stuff of navigating round life as Muslim people see it - a kind of highway code. To live close to Muslim people is to realise how materialist life in the West has become; for twenty-first century people, there is nothing beyond what you can see and touch. Not so for my Muslim friend, who lives in a spiritual world which needs to be taken into account. There are spirits (djinns) and angels of different kinds, there are spiritual forces that have to be avoided or harnessed, there are individuals who possess spiritual power and can use it to benefit or damage others. In all the Muslim societies I have lived in, magic and the occult have been endemic. It is so important to remind ourselves constantly that this is the spiritual world in which our Muslim friends live.

Before a Western mother crosses the road with her children, she will hold their hands and look carefully to see if it is safe to cross. If a bus is coming she will wait. A Muslim mother will protect her children from the 'evil eye' in the same way. She may take steps to protect them by not allowing her girls to be too well-dressed, pretty, or clean, and so avoid compliments which, coming from envy, will expose them to the 'evil eye'. In the same way she will be careful how she compliments other children. If she is pregnant she will take special care of her unborn baby, as now she is more susceptible. The family that keeps its little girls messy and unwashed is not feckless; they are protecting their girls against the evil eye, and the danger that pretty little girls might incur the envy of a relative or neighbour.

Shabana was born and brought up in England, though her family is from Pakistan. Mohammed, her very handsome and good-looking husband, had shockingly high blood pressure. From time to time he and I would cross swords about why he refused to take any medicines. I would remonstrate without effect. Finally, as I had feared, he had a serious stroke and was paralysed down one side.

During his long and difficult recovery period I would visit the family.

"You know," said Shabana, "You think Mohammed had his stroke because he didn't take anything for his blood pressure. Well you're wrong! It's Hudda, the lady up the road. She saw Mohammed painting the gate and she envied him for his good looks. She gave him the eye and now look at him."

"So what are you doing about it?"

"We went to the pir. He gave us this." Shabana points to a taweez that Mohammed is wearing. "That's why he's getting better. She came to visit us the other day; when she'd gone we remembered where she had stepped and drove a nail into the floor - there!." She points. A nail head is visible among the carpet fibres.

Mohammed hasn't said anything. Like so many men, he isn't sure he believes all this, but is prepared to go along with it. He has started to take medicines to lower his blood pressure, but he is also wearing a taweez. The magic and occult practice is mostly in the hands of his wife and other women in his family, but he is wearing one, 'just in case'.

Magic and occult beliefs are, for many people, what makes the world go round. They are a much closer reality than classic Islamic doctrine, and much more deeply embedded. In fact most of these beliefs predate Islam by centuries. Most families are involved in some way and to reach this at 'gut' level is to make contact with something far more basic than the tenets of their religion, even though these are held to with great sincerity. There are some imams who have baraka - who are known to have spiritual powers - but within the family the magic is almost invariably in the hands of women. This is true despite - or almost certainly because of – the fact that women have so little power elsewhere. In some areas of northern Sudan the women are steeped in magic and occult practices. They are able to conjure up 'zar' spirits, a routine feature at weddings. The men have little to do with these goings-on, as it is within the female sphere of influence and control. Although all these women will call themselves Muslims, they know very little of formal Islam. The occult is a far more profound influence on them. The key is to listen and ask questions to find just how deep that influence is, and how much it affects them.

Unlike Islamic doctrine, magic and occult beliefs are very diverse, both in their content and in the importance that is attached to them. Whatever its character however, practicing the occult is dabbling in the supernatural and therefore dangerous. It is also completely amoral.

Relationships, women and family life

The place of women in Islam is the subject of many stereotypes. Fortunately, if you visit your Muslim friends the place of women in each individual home will become apparent, and the idea that men are always predominant and women subservient will be quickly modified.

Mohammed is a prominent imam who enjoys significant status among other men and at the mosque. At home his position changes. His wife, physically much bigger than he, is also bigger in personality. At home, she is in charge. As Mohammed crosses his doorstep he seems to visibly decrease in size. The same can be said of very many homes, where the situation resembles the southern European model of the powerful 'Mama'. Rosina, a powerful elderly lady, lived close to the surgery. She knew that the doors closed punctually at 6pm; anybody already inside would be seen, and latecomers would have to wait until the next day. At about 7pm she would come past the doctor's window. Not bothering to come to the front door, Rosina would bang on the glass loudly, ignoring the consultation going on within. After many attempts at asking her to modify her behaviour, I realised that resistance was useless. I would capitulate and ask for her (and several other family members) to be let in. Even a deputation to her home was of no avail. Smiling, she promised to come on time in future, but as I leave her son shrugged: "Sorry Doc," he said ruefully, "Grandma rules the roost round here and there aren't going to be any changes any time soon!"

It is helpful to look at the family diagrammatically. There are 'male spaces' and 'female spaces', where each gender has the right to exert power. If these spaces are regarded as circles they may intersect to a greater or lesser extent, with the area where they overlap being the area where men and women associate freely together. In Western society the circles overlap, say, this much:

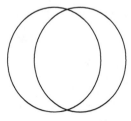

To a large extent men and women live, work and associate together. Spaces where men or women exert no power or have no right of entry are comparatively few. It might be suggested that the circles are overlapping more and more as exclusively male spaces such as Royal Naval submarines and London clubs are conceded to (or invaded by, according to one's point of view) women.

In Muslim societies, these circles overlap much less, and women and men live much more separate lives, more like this:

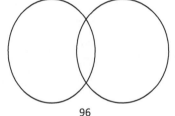

Women sit in separate spaces in the mosque and are accorded lower status when they are there. Men are accorded power status in the street and other public places, a status symbolised by men walking a few paces in front of their wives. In some Muslim countries such as Yemen, women have been regarded as 'loose' if they go out into the streets alone. However, as we have seen, in the area of magic women exert enormous power. They also exert power over men when they are in the home. There are large areas where men and women operate either exclusively or dominantly.

How this works out in each community and family, and how much it is changing over time, is for you to work out for yourself. It is an antidote to the stereotype that in Islam woman all women are oppressed; the reality is much more complicated, varied and subject to change. Moreover, the power or weakness of personalities always moderates cultural 'rules' one way or another.

For Pakistani Muslims in UK, the home and private life is a female space; the mosque and public life is, by and large, a male space. As a family doctor I was regarded as sexless; a doubtful privilege, but one that afforded me access to the female space in the home. This was strictly limited to my role as a GP. The private heart domain of Muslim women is accessible to women only. We have already seen that women have far more power in 'spiritual' matters like the occult and magic, which makes the role of women absolutely crucial when it comes to sharing the Good News. Among the Beja of northern Sudan, the women are profoundly oppressed and underprivileged, yet even there the men of the family have to leave the family home in daylight hours, during which the women have the right to this space for themselves.

Marriage

A young woman arrives from an Asian country. A marriage has been arranged to a young man, probably a cousin, whom she may never have seen, and she has had no say in whether she comes to Britain or not. She will probably move into the home of her in-laws, as the idea of a new home for a new marriage relationship is entirely foreign to many Asian cultures. She may also find that her new husband has a very tight relationship with his mother, and he will implicitly do what she asks - or says - rather than listen to his wife. On the other hand, a young man or woman brought up in the West is likely to look for a Western-style partnership rather than the parent-dominated marriage that his or her mother has been led to expect from her Asian upbringing.

Nazreen was 17 years old when she arrived as Shafiq's bride. It was a miserable October and she found the rain and long dark nights desperately depressing. Shafiq's sisters, two trendy teenage girls, did their best to take care of her, and Shafiq's mother was kindness itself. Nevertheless Nazreen had a very difficult first winter. Shafiq, born and bred in the Midlands, was looking for a Western-style relationship, and his illiterate bride, steeped in the traditions of her mountain village, found this entirely outside her sphere of reference. Shafiq's mother, although very considerate, expected Nazreen to spend the bulk of her time in the female circle, and expected that as his mother, she herself would continue to be the most important woman in Shafiq's life, remaining his confidante and adviser. She saw Nazreen's role as that of a junior woman in the female family hierarchy, whose main task was to get pregnant as soon as possible. The young couple were in a quandary; Shafiq was torn between his mother's expectations and his own, and Nazreen was culturally ill-equipped for a relationship with her husband in the Western sense, and would rather have settled for the role that her mother-in-law saw for her.

The odds stacked up against such a relationship are great. The girl may retreat into female relationships. The young man might, in emotional frustration, look for another relationship outside the home. It is heartwarming to see how many couples work hard at overcoming these huge cultural difficulties.

Ali Sultan came from Pakistan to marry Noor, a feisty Brummie girl. They argued and fought incessantly from day one. Noor was furious that Ali wanted her to walk behind him in the street like her parents did in the traditional Pakistani way. Ali was outraged and confused that his wife did not wish to show him respect in the manner that he had been brought up to assume was his due as a husband. Noor felt that as a younger-generation Asian woman, to walk behind her husband would be a sign of public humiliation and a symbol of just the kind of relationship that she did not want. They often came to blows. "How dare he treat me like a servant," she shouted, "He's got to learn we aren't in Pakistan now." As the months went on a truce emerged. They would walk side by side unless they were going to a wedding or other formal event.

I would see them walking happily together. Then one day I caught sight of them both dressed to kill in their finery on their way to a wedding, and Noor was walking three paces behind Ali in the time-honoured way. Peace was arrived at after hard bargaining and with give and take on both sides. In due course a happy relationship developed.

Marriage in most Muslim societies is radically different from what we are used to in the west. The marriage relationship does not hold the central place that it holds (even now) in British family life, and many marriages are arranged, frequently between partners from different countries, for distinct family and financial reasons. In Islamic law a woman must have a half share along with her brothers in their father's will, so a marriage within the larger family will preserve the family finances intact. Men often have very strong and unhealthy relationships with their mothers which continue after marriage, putting great strain on their relationship with their wives. Often a newly married couple will move into the home of the mother-in-law, as Nazreen and Shafiq had done, and there is little sense of 'leaving and cleaving', or the establishment of a new unit with a new identity and a new home. More importantly there are major changes taking place within families who are adapting in their own way to massive cultural shifts, and are very conscious that the old ways often cause much misery in a British context.

Your own friends will tell you about their relationships and families when you have gained their confidence, and your own observation will tell you volumes.

Seclusion and the veil

The full veil, or niqab, is becoming commoner in Britain. Previously a symbol of the social and economic status of the husband, it has only recently become a political and religious weapon. The black and sombre appearance does what it is supposed to do: completely conceal the individual behind, who is probably wearing a Hard Rock Café t-shirt underneath.

Previously the veil was hardly used by the Pakistani community, women instead using the 'dapatta' - the white shawl with which they covered their heads, and which they would use to reveal or cover part of their faces. This form of dress symbolised their obedience to the family mores, and upheld the honour of the man of the family. When British-born Muslim women attended our surgery wearing niqab, they would invariably toss it back the moment they walked into the consultation room. Now things are different; when I worked in the north of England there were a number of women wearing niqab who preferred to keep it on. There is obviously a problem here, as the person wearing the veil can see you, but you cannot see her.

I suggested to Intisar that as we had met three times she might like to remove her veil. She indicated that she preferred to stay as she was and I reluctantly continued.

"So what's the problem?" I asked.

"My throat," she said, "It's killing me."

"Well," I said, trying to be tactful, "We aren't going to get very far if I can't take a look!"

She burst out laughing, threw back her veil and gave me a first-rate view of her tonsils.

The veil hides a world of hypocrisy. In Sudan I was twice touched most inappropriately in the street by women wearing niqab. To the hilarity of shopkeepers and bystanders, I was chased through the market in Port Sudan by half a dozen veiled women from the Rashaida, an Arab nomadic tribe, all desperate to sell me their jewelry. My personal experience leads me to take the religious rhetoric of modesty with a very large pinch of salt.

The niqab is also deeply unpopular with many Muslim women themselves, who feel as confused by it as native British people do. To them, the implication is that the lady requires protection from the people she is talking to and working among; were this not so, she would do as she does at home, a 'safe' female space where she is exposed only to her husband and brothers, and not wear it. Muslim women who go unveiled often feel that it is being inferred that they are not as good Muslims as their veiled sisters are, and feel pushed into a more extreme religious position. If we assume that a lady is wearing niqab because of personal and individual piety or devotion, we are imputing to her an outlook that is actually not at all Islamic. Someone wearing a Manchester United shirt is wearing it because they are a part of the team, or a supporter of it. Niqab is exactly the same. It indicates solidarity not individuality, though of course a Westernised woman may well superimpose her individualism on her religion and wear niqab for that reason. An indigenous British lady who becomes a Muslim may also wear this dress to show her own personal devotion to Islam.

For a Christian who wants to get close to Muslim people, the most important thing is not to take the veil at face value. There is a living, breathing, probably giggling woman behind that piece of cloth, and it is this person we must address if needed, not the black hooded figure you can actually see. Of course this applies mostly to women, who can start to ask why the veil is being worn. If there is a relationship between you, and the woman feels she can talk to you, there will be all kinds of surprising answers. 'I do it for a quiet life', 'My brother goes on at me if I don't', and 'Look, I wear this, and underneath I do my own head work,' are just a handful of answers I have heard.

As I have said, women do not wear the veil at home, and in fact many women change behaviour radically between home and the workplace. Na'amin was a most confident and efficient hospital manager and obviously loved her job. She was often bouncy and noisy.

"Do you behave like this at home?" I asked one day. "How does your family cope with you?"

"You don't think I behave like this at home, do you?" she laughed, "I could never! You should see me, I make food for my brothers, I serve them, I keep quiet, I really act up!"[17]

"Which is the real you?"

She was quiet for a moment. "Oh," she said, "This is the real me, here."

---

[17] Vreeda de Stuers documents the different behaviour of women in front of their husbands and close male relatives compared with that adopted when they were with other women. Vreeda de Stuers; *Parda: a Study of Muslim Women's Life in Northern India* (Assen: Van Gorcum, 1968)

Women who came to our surgery routinely behaved in front of their husbands and other male relations in a reserved and subdued manner. When alone, they explained that there was a mode of behaviour that was expected of a good wife while in the presence of her husband, particularly in front of men from outside their immediate family. When I started work at the surgery, women invariably came with their husbands or brothers. They would sit without speaking, heads bowed, faces partially covered with their dapattas. Often they spoke little or no English.

"Could you explain what we've just discussed?" I once said to a husband, when we had been through a consultation; I was horribly conscious that his wife had been a silent and uninvolved presence, even though the problem was hers alone.

"I'll explain it to her when we get home," was the reply.

After a month or two, husbands came less and less. Perhaps they had decided that I was not dangerous after all. Away from their men, women chatted, laughed and behaved normally. Some knew much more English than I had ever guessed from our previous chaperoned encounters. "Don't tell my husband I speak English!" one said. As a man outside their culture I didn't 'count', and women often said that, because of this, they were able to behave 'normally'.

As time went on, more and more women seemed to come to the surgery as a place of escape from the constraints of their culture. Although the veil was little used in Pakistan, seclusion (purdah) had been a prominent part of life there, and many women hated it. "It was wonderful when we women were there in the village," an elderly lady remarked, "and all the men were away in Birmingham. We ran all the farms, the shops and the businesses ourselves, we did what we liked and there was no purdah. And then we had to come here!"

Most married women were only able to leave home with the permission of their mother-in-law; but an exception was that they were able to visit the surgery, and many took full advantage of this. If Tabassum and her five children came through the door we knew that Shagufta and her brood would not be far behind. They would have an hour or two chatting and playing in the waiting room before seeing the doctor and leaving. When we (unsuccessfully) tried to introduce an appointments system many women were horrified; "but how do you think we are going to meet our friends?" said Tabassum.

Seclusion is deeply entrenched in South Asian Muslim culture. Many young men expressed the opinion that when they were married a degree of seclusion would result. "I don't want my wife going about like English women," said Khalid to me one day. When I asked why this should be, he thought for moment. "It's our religion," he said. A year or two later Khalid married a spirited, good-looking and very trendy girl. I remember Azra well, as she wore the longest ear rings I have ever seen. Azra underwent enforced seclusion above a hardware shop and for two years she was a virtual prisoner. The experiment eventually came to an end, but not before much heartbreak, conflict and some violence. Noreen and Khalid's experience illustrates the way culture from 'home' interacts with culture in Britain, and how change gradually occurs. It also shows how Muslim people do not compartmentalise their lives into 'religion' and 'culture'.

Honour and shame

The concept of honour is hard to grasp, as it has virtually disappeared from Western cultural life; yet it is key to understanding much Muslim behaviour.

We have seen earlier how the honour of the Prophet is close to the heart of the devout Muslim, and how behaviour is often motivated by a passion - or a need to be seen to be passionate - for the defence of the name of Muhammad. A Muslim friend said to me, "Say what you like about God. But be careful what you say about the Prophet!" This really puts it in a nutshell. Muslims are often far more sensitive about their Prophet than about God.

The culture of shame extends deep into family life. Older English people may remember how unmarried girls who became pregnant were thrown out of their homes, and we now generally recoil with horror at such cruelty. It usually occurred because the 'family honour' had been violated, and very much the same idea prevails today in Muslim families. The honour of a family man as 'head of the family' depends on the chastity of 'his women', and their obedience; especially the importance of the fact that each of them should marry the man he has chosen for her. This is frequently a cousin, though actually the choice is usually not made by the man himself but by his wife, who as a woman has access to likely marriage partners.

Yusif and Abdul Rashid were two brothers caught up in an operetta-like scenario that would have been hilarious as fiction had it not been deeply painful in reality. As happens in many families, they had been betrothed from childhood to two sisters, Sultana and Salima respectively. As they grew up, Abdul Rashid fell for Sultana, the 'wrong' sister, and a longstanding secret love affair ensued. When they became adults the date of the two marriages was fixed. As the day drew near the truth emerged when they were discovered in the act of making love. The parents of both couples were traumatised. While doing their best to understand, allowing the pair to marry was not an option. Surprisingly it was not really an option for Abdul Rashid either, who felt that as a 'good Muslim' he should honour his father, rather than follow his own inclination. When I last saw him, Abdul Rashid and Salima were sincerely and diligently trying to forge a relationship against their natural inclinations. Here were second-generation Pakistani Muslims, sharing the honour culture with their parents, and trying to be dutiful children. This family did not distinguish between 'culture' and Islam, never for one moment thinking that the honour issue was 'culture' rather than 'religion'. It is an example of the integration that is such a feature of Muslim thinking. A man might wear a Western suit to work in the week but wear Islamic clothing to go to the mosque on Friday, as we saw previously with our parable of Ahmed in Chapter 1. To a Westerner, he is merely wearing traditional Pakistani clothing, but that is not at all what he sees himself doing.

The arranged marriage issue, however, is directly Islamic insofar as it relates to inheritance. As I have noted above, Muslim law dictates that a half-share of an inheritance goes to a daughter. Marrying into close family ensures that any inheritance she receives also stays within the extended family. Moreover, there is a strong belief that 'duty of care' continues even after marriage; the close family tie enables her brothers to exercise some protection over their sister, even in the new relationship.

The honour culture in the home is in some ways becoming less demanding, and many older-generation parents are thinking hard about allowing their children to marry. However the honour culture deeply affects families when a family member becomes interested in the Christian Gospel or decides to follow Christ. If this remains secret an amazing tolerance can result. A more likely scenario is the one I have referred to earlier. For a Muslim to become a Christian is an act of treachery to his or her family, partly because most Muslims don't actually know what a 'Christian' is, and the word itself brings up a host of completely erroneous ideas. To say that one has become a 'follower of the prophet Jesus' or a 'disciple of Issa the Messiah' may ease things, and might even lead to curiosity about what this actually means, but it is true to say that a Muslim who decides to follow Christ, however it is put, is usually seen as violating his or her family's honour. We have seen how Jamil's family was deeply disrupted by his decision to follow Christ, with his father outraged and his mother driven to meeting him secretly.

Another important aspect of honour is how it is seen in individual behaviour, and it seems that this is especially so with men. In a conversation with a young Muslim it will be most important to him that he be seen, by his peers and by you yourself, as a good and upright Muslim, and this will strongly influence the way he behaves. It is possible that he will develop a 'persona' to portray himself as such to others - and indeed to himself. The result might be an impression of him as an aggressive and devout Muslim that is actually very far from the truth. It is most important that we do not speak to this persona, and in so doing reinforce it, but instead speak to the real person behind it. We can do this by forming a relationship and seeing the person on his own - and by simply not being taken in by the display.

Identity

It is obvious from everything that we have looked at so far that Islam fosters a very powerful sense of belonging and identity, both corporate and personal. When we talk to our Muslim friends about their life and their faith, we are not looking at something objective but rather touching on something very profound. Any questioning of Islam can be very threatening, and we need to keep in mind that we are engaging hugely powerful emotions.

Islam's self-image

The symbols of Islamic presence are prominent and imposing. Mosques are tall; clothing referred to as 'Islamic' is radically different from other British modes of dress. Young men wear beards brushed out to make the most of their size. Islam has a prominent place in the media quite unlike that of any other minority ethnic group or religion. Some Muslims talk of Islam in what you may see as an aggressive manner, and will define it for you assertively. It is important that we do not uncritically adopt this view of Islam, not least because so much of Islamic life is unseen. Our own view should come out of a certain detachment, informed by our own study and observation, our own experience, our own relationships, by the Holy Spirit and by prayer.

We have moved a long way from classical Islam. If we are to relate well to our Muslim friends, we must do them the honour of being interested not only in their beliefs but in all the other preoccupations of their lives. We must also honour them by seeing them as they are within the Islamic biosphere, rather than as theological texts or indeed as they themselves present themselves to us. We discover and understand how to do this through our loving relationships, our observation, our unfeigned interest, our tactful questioning, and our listening to the varied answers we will receive.

Formal Islam does not address the needs of the heart, and Muslims must look elsewhere for these needs to be met, whether legitimate in Islamic theology or not. We need to take the trouble to lovingly observe our friends, and show ourselves interested in the deep things of their lives. When we see things at 'gut' level we are far closer to forming deep relationships, and it is here that the Good News of Christ can find a ready listening ear.

Chapter 6

Pitfalls

The language barrier

This Sunday, imagine you are with an 'international' friend whom you have invited to church, or who perhaps has invited herself. Take a look at the service sheet you were both given with a smile at the door. During a boring moment, take your biro and circle the words that your friend will find incomprehensible.

Even before you have left the dateline you will have underlined 'Advent' or 'Pentecost'. 'Baptism' is a little further down. 'Salvation', 'hymn', 'psalm', 'congregation', 'catholic' and 'incarnate' might follow.

Now circle the words that your friend may think she understands, but in fact doesn't because their meanings are entirely different from what she is used to. These come thick and fast. 'Kingdom', 'love', 'passion', 'word', 'cross', 'Jesus'; the list goes on and on. If 'Zion' is mentioned, your friend, if she is a Muslim, might be seething quietly or even have stormed out. And what is all this talk of a lamb? It is probable that your church's service sheet contains only two sentences that can be relied on as comprehensible to a person not immersed in Christian culture: "Please be sure to switch off your mobile phone", and the final invitation to coffee afterwards.

In church we do not speak English, we speak Church-ese. Your friend will not have a clue as to what we are all talking about. "Oh yes," said our Chinese neighbour after one service, "I understand now what 'Easter' means; it is something to do with Christianity!"

No work, sport, academic discipline or other walk of life is without its jargon, and the Church is no exception. Some of it is found in this book, which contains words like 'Gospel' that are short for things it would take many more words to explain properly. To use all those words repeatedly instead of saying 'Gospel' would be tedious and unnecessary - as long as we are sure that we are talking to people who speak the same language. The trouble comes when, like your friend above, someone comes into the church and is quite excluded and confused because of a breakdown in communication.

Before we can go on to discuss any kind of sharing the Good News we need to grapple with the language problem, but we also need to make ourselves aware of some huge advantages that we have as Christians that narrow the gap between ourselves and Muslims, making genuine contact and communication possible in unique ways.

One word, two meanings

When we talk, we depend on the fact that the words we use mean pretty well the same thing to ourselves and to our hearers. When this breaks down, and it is obvious that it has broken down, the results are often hilarious. It is far more serious when there is a breakdown in meaning and we are unaware of it - when the words we are using mean one thing to ourselves and something entirely different to our hearers, and yet we all blissfully continue thinking we mean the same thing.

When I use the word 'God', I will have a very clear and detailed meaning for what I am saying in my own head. My Muslim friend has equally clear ideas in his own head as to what 'God' means. When we talk, we may agree that 'God is one'. Here, at least, we have something in common; here we can start to build bridges. We understand each other, and even though we disagree about many things, we are communicating. Well-meaning men and women point to God's unity as a point of contact where we can build relationships. Islam is not so very far from faith in Christ they say; we all believe in one God.

Well actually, no. It is precisely here, at the point of the unity of God and his oneness, that we are furthest apart. We have discussed the character of the God of Islam, and his oneness, in an earlier chapter. The God of Islam is profoundly different from the Father of Jesus Christ.

The Gospel of Christ means nothing if it is not built solidly on the foundation of the character of God, revealed by the entire body of scripture - the words of God and his actions, the relationships he forms with men and women and his dealings with them. If I share the Good News with men and women whose view of God is other than that revealed in the Bible, that Good News is going to be meaningless and incomprehensible. It is also going to be wrong! It is as though I was trying to use a Morris Minor workshop manual to repair my Bentley. The character of God in Islam is seriously different from the biblical character of God. As we have seen earlier, the oneness of God in Islam is its central tenet. God is isolated and alone in his inviolable unity, and this essentially precludes intimacy and relationship - certainly and specifically, it precludes him having a son. The God of the Bible is indeed one, but in a completely different way. His oneness encompasses the great truth of the Trinity. Far from being a point of connection and mutual understanding, the oneness of God is the point at which our divisions are most marked.

When I use the word 'Jesus', what is happening in my own mind? If I have been a Christian for a few years there will be a cloud of very rich meaning around this word. As with my idea of God, there will be a composite picture that has been built up through my Bible reading, through interaction with other Christians and through many sermons and much teaching (both exciting and dull). Words such as 'saviour', ' redeemer', 'son' and many others, each one with their own cloud of meaning, will tumble through my consciousness. Then there are the pictures in my imagination of Jesus during his earthly life, my own experience of God and my own personal story which is the direct experience of his work in me, and there is the sheer length of time that I have known him, which may be brief, or may be a lifetime. There is my immense gratitude for what he has done for me, a sense of his love and involvement in my life.

It may be a far from perfect picture - in fact it may actually be wrong in parts - but it is detailed, highly complicated, rich, and full of deep feeling and personal involvement. Furthermore, I will think of Jesus often; he will be the home of my thoughts. If I use the word 'Jesus', I am more or less consciously communicating all of this, and my Christian friends have an experience of Jesus that is not identical to mine, but there is enough overlap to make genuine communication possible.

But if I use the word 'Jesus' to my Muslim friend, what will come into his mind? Not the same thing at all. It will be safe to assume that he won't have had much involvement with this word very much, if at all, and if he has it is unlikely to have been through the Bible. There will be no personal experience, no emotional involvement, and no gratitude. Furthermore, it is not likely that he will think of Jesus very often; Jesus is, or has been, peripheral to his life. His focus has been elsewhere. It is true that Jesus has a very high place in Islam. Many have told me, "Yes, we Muslims love Jesus," but my Muslim friend will also have many erroneous ideas about him and they may be very strongly held. He will have no hesitation in telling me that Jesus is not the son of God. If I argue with him and say that he is, our misunderstanding is compounded. He will be outraged that God, who is one and cannot have a son, is held to be a father. Communication goes out of the window and confusion reigns supreme.

The problem is that we are using words that have widely differing meanings to each of us. The word 'Jesus', like the word 'God', has one meaning for me, and an entirely different meaning for my Muslim friend. If I argue that Jesus is the son of God, in terms of what these words mean in Islam and in his own head, I am actually saying something that is completely untrue. He will be quite right to deny this. In Islamic terms Jesus, or Issa as he is referred to in Islam, is definitely not the son of God, and I am entirely wrong to try to persuade him that he is. This statement is only true if 'God' is the God of the Bible, 'Jesus' is the Jesus of the New Testament, and 'son' has a fully biblical meaning. The Good News is not about words, it is about the truths that these words represent. It is about Jesus the person, the one who says "I am the truth".

The language difficulty does not stop here. It is my greatest desire that my friend should become a Christian, and I have a very clear idea of what this means to me. But what does my friend think a 'Christian' is, and what does 'becoming a Christian' mean to him? If I take steps to find out I may be horrified at the misconceptions in his mind. What I perceive as resistance might just be an unwillingness to do or become something that was in any case very far from what I think he should be doing or becoming. Many

Muslims have only a very vague and inaccurate idea of what Christianity is, and have a very hard time grasping that no one is born a Christian and instead that all Christians will have *become* Christians. This arises out of the very strong sense of the family of Islam, the 'Umma' that he or she has been born into; that every child becomes a Muslim when the first words he or she hears are the 'Shehada', the words 'There is no God but Allah, and Muhammad is his Prophet' whispered into their ears immediately after birth. If you are in a Muslim family then you are a Muslim. That there is any choice involved does not occur to him for a moment. 'Becoming' a Muslim is an alien idea, and many feel that Westerners cannot really become true Muslims.

Furthermore, Islam identifies and defines itself very strongly as 'religion' and it is natural that Muslims should look at Christianity and assume that it is another religion of the same order, but different - and inferior! This may be a natural assumption, but it is entirely incorrect. Your friend may assume that what you want him to do is 'change his religion'; but you do not see it like this at all.

In fact 'religion' is a perfect example of the kind of word that confuses while pretending to clarify. Such phrases as 'the three Abrahamic religions' suggest an affinity that does not in fact exist - it's politically useful but owes little to either history or theology.

I have asked many of my Muslim friends if Islam is religion. They are immediately at ease in affirming that Islam is 'deen' (religion), and they use the word frequently. But 'religion' is a word that is notoriously difficult to define. Cantwell Smith talks about 'an overt system of beliefs, practices and values, related to a particular community', and it seems safe to say that most Muslims I have talked to would actually be happier if we said that their religion is 'what Islam is'.

I would argue that although Christianity might be 'an overt system of beliefs, practices and values', this does not get to the heart of things at all. It may be seen as such from the outside, but as a description this entirely misses the point, and it is certainly not 'Good News' to portray faith in Christ in such terms.

No. Christianity is a relationship with a living person. We believe in no disembodied 'truths' that are not in him who said "I am the truth". We believe in no objective practices that are not in he who said "I am the way". Our relationship depends on what and who Jesus himself is, what he has done for us and his attitude of love to us. "We love him because he first loved us."(1 John ch.4 v.19)

It is for this reason that I suggest we use the word 'relationship' for what Christianity is, and that we use it where our Muslim friend uses the word 'religion'. It will avoid assuming points of contact where none exist, and it will highlight the contrast between Islam and Christianity. It leads us straight to the heart of the Good News - which is not a series of facts and assertions, however true in themselves, but an introduction and a call to a relationship with a person.

We can go on and on with the words that we use; 'sin', 'love', 'prayer', 'father' - all have radically different meanings. Even the word 'fundamentalist' is used entirely differently by Muslims, Christians and secularists - to ongoing and daily confusion. Furthermore the problem is the same from the Muslim angle. Remember that when your Muslim friend uses the name 'Muhammad' it has a rich personal and emotional aura for him, every bit as deep and complex as the word 'Jesus' has for you.

And it isn't words only. I once asked a young man why he was wearing a taweez. "For the same reason you're wearing that, Doc," he said, pointing to the tiny cross on the collar of my jacket.

That was the last time I ever wore that little cross. I did not want it to be read as a magic talisman. That episode indicated forcefully me to how a message that I intended to convey could be so fatally misinterpreted.

Do not despair however; communication is entirely possible if we take steps to overcome this difficulty, and we can do that in four ways.

The first step is simply for us and our Muslim friends to become aware of this difficulty, and become able to have a good laugh over it. Of course we do not need to confront this problem immediately; but we ourselves need to be very aware of it at the outset. It may be far less confrontational to adopt a more gradual approach. You may argue fiercely about the character of God but this is far better than assuming that the two of you mean the same thing when you say the word 'God'.

Secondly, we need to use terms that are not instantly misunderstood. 'Christian' is such a loaded term that it best avoided. The word 'disciple' or 'murid' is familiar in Birmingham, Bradford and places where pirs have their murids, and the concept and relationship is not dissimilar, so try using terms such as 'disciples of Jesus' or 'followers of Jesus', or of 'the Messiah' - a very useful term, since Muslims all acknowledge that Jesus is the Messiah, but 'Messiah' as a term is nowhere explained, and is therefore less full of wrong assumptions. Or for Jesus himself one might use the term 'Jesus the Messiah', or perhaps use the name by which Jesus is referred to in Islam: 'Issa', 'Issa Massih', 'Issa bin Mariam', or even "Sayidna Issa", Our Lord Issa. Devout Muslims will say the Salawaat - "blessings and peace be upon him" - when they mention the Prophet's name. You might like to say "blessings and peace be upon us" when you mention the name of Jesus, at least on the first couple of occasions. Your friend might be interested in the contrast and wonder why we do not ask for blessings on him but on ourselves. You, on the other hand, might well ask why, in view of his prophethood, your friend - and for that matter Muslims all over the world - are praying for him. Is it not a foregone conclusion that he is accepted by God and does not need to be prayed for?

All this will in any case need discussion and explanation. It might be good to say that Christianity is not a 'religion' at all, but a relationship - a rescue service set up by God. Emphasise the differences between Islam and Christianity. Hungry Muslims who have searched their own faith and found it unable to meet the needs of their own hearts are betrayed by an assurance that Islam and Christianity are not that different after all.

Thirdly we need to spend time asking our friend what he understands by words like 'Jesus' and some of the other words that we may be using as we talk together. This has the great benefit of increasing understanding and goes some way towards clearing the confusion.

The final and fourth step is by far the most important. Where do we get a lucid, exciting and biblical picture of who God is, what he is like, his plan for his son, who Jesus is, what he says, what he thinks about us and his amazing rescue plan? In the Bible! Reading the Bible with our Muslim friend will slowly and effectively introduce Jesus as he really is.

History

As we sit down and talk with our Muslim friends there is a huge historical backdrop of conflict that is present, whether we like it or not. We need to take into account the history of the Crusades, the rapid military expansion of Islam into Europe that preceded it, and the centuries of conflict between what are seen, rightly or wrongly, as monolithic blocs: 'Christianity' and 'Islam'. (There have of course been years and years of relatively peaceful co-existence too). There is the imperialism of the last two centuries, during which the Western nations carved up the Middle East into units that suited their own interests, leaving a huge and lasting legacy of problems. There is the notorious Balfour Declaration, seen by Arabs universally as a self-interested betrayal of the interests of Palestinians of any and all faiths. We as Christians can never adopt the moral high ground when discussing these matters.

Westerners are often only dimly conscious of the details of these events, but it is certain that they will loom much larger in the mind of your Muslim friend. Muslims tend to be much more conscious of their history than we are, and more importantly, their perspective is often stunningly different from our own. Ask your Muslim friend about these great historical events. You may hardly recognise them from her perspective. But your job is not to argue - it is to understand and appreciate where they are coming from.

Politics

The running sore of the Israel-Palestine situation engages the passion of many who have nothing practical to do with it. The initiation and perpetuation of this evil is laid at the door of Britain and the United States respectively. With the sudden emergence of Islamic State (or ISIS, ISIL, or Daesh) there is a heightened anxiety and awareness of the very active and tense political arena that we are entering when we interact with our Muslim friends. In fact, there may be a quiet (or noisy) tape running in the head of your friend which says something like this:

> Christians have always seen Muslims as the enemy.

> Christians and the West have exploited and oppressed Muslims.

> Christians support Israel, so we Muslims are definitely seen as second class.

At some stage we may need to identify this. We also - and much more importantly - need to identify these attitudes in ourselves and deal with them. How is it possible to reach Muslim people with such a cloud of influences that predisposes antagonism between us before we even speak?

Fortunately there is, as ever, an answer. These attitudes flourish where there is little contact between Muslims and Christians, and where there are assumptions but no enquiry, a lack of direct and searching communication. Where there are maturing relationships and trust is being established, these matters can come to the foreground. You might be able to offer an apology for wrongs that have been inflicted in the past. It is humbling how your apology on behalf of people you never knew, regarding a matter you are in no way personally responsible for, can affect a relationship for the better and clear away barriers. Don't expect reciprocity, and don't get into an argument. Our aim is to remove barriers to the sharing of the Good News, not to score points. It is most unlikely that your friend will consider apologising for anything done in the name of Islam, and may be astounded that you should offer such an apology for your own predecessors. Your apology will show nothing but grace. You will have turned a pitfall into an open door.

Current events

Islam has a huge profile in the media from day to day. There are regular warnings of possible or probable terrorist events. The day after the July 7th bombings in London, I went to work in my surgery. The bombings were never mentioned by any Muslim that I met, that day or subsequently. Any conversation about it was as a result of me bringing up the subject myself. I have talked about terrorism and suicide bombings on various occasions and the response has been varied and complex, but there has never been a shadow over our conversation or a suggestion that there was an impenetrable barrier.

This book does not attempt to address the issues around modern 'Islamism', but their appearance has caused a groundswell of anxiety among many Muslims whom I have talked to, which has been particularly heightened with the appearance of IS. Many feel a tension in the fact that they are part of an ideology that can produce such devastation. They are bound to Islam but are very uneasy about some aspects of it. It is this very political turmoil that stimulates inner thought, the 'heart work' that many Muslims are doing privately. I have asked quite a number of friends, both in UK and in the Middle East, to tell me what they see as the defining difference between IS and 'normal' Islam. No one has been able to provide an answer - to the obvious distress of some. Many take refuge in denial. "Islam is a peaceful religion," is something we hear repeatedly, and many Muslims actually believe this: they have ignored the warlike origins of their religion, the fierce utterances of their Prophet, the laws that militate against any attempt to embrace any other faith and the total absence in their scriptures of any guidance as to how to live in cooperation with those of another culture or faith. On the other hand my experience is that there are many within Islam who are doing a lot of internal heart work.

The violent events of the present day will be a constant spur to their inner searchings.

In fact we need to see the political dimension not as a disadvantage but as a very real advantage. In what Muslim country is an individual Muslim free to explore the Christian faith safely? Few, if any. Muslims have to resort to endless subterfuge, and encounter much personal difficulty and danger from family and friends if they do not. In what Muslim country can Christians worship and share their faith with freedom? As an expatriate worker in Sudan I enjoyed remarkable liberty, but at the same time I have seen my Sudanese friends subjected to considerable harassment. Evangelism without immediate results may be tolerated, but when men and women start following Christ there is often an explosive reaction.

In Britain, on the other hand, Muslims have complete political freedom to explore Christianity, and Christians have a corresponding freedom to share the Gospel with Muslims. This does not mean that Muslims do not experience pressure from their families - and perhaps this is actually more powerful in Europe than in 'home' countries such as Pakistan or Yemen. When a community is in the minority it is more concerned about maintaining its boundaries.

Freedom of speech is a priceless gift and privilege. All those who live in Britain are entitled to speak freely of their faith in any situation; Muslims find themselves far freer to worship and talk to others of Islam in Britain than Christians do in majority-Muslim countries. In Britain, no Christian should find themselves in any situation where they are not allowed to pray or share the Good News with anyone, Muslim or otherwise, and any attempt to prevent this should be challenged. If you are asked - or told - that you should not talk of Christianity in, for instance, your work situation, ask for it in writing!

Sensitivity

Nevertheless there have been attempts to curtail this freedom of speech. There is a sensitivity to criticism within Islam that is highly effective at silencing comment, and which sometimes engenders an anxiety among those who work with Muslims that somehow they are going to cause offence. In public life this sensitivity has communicated itself so effectively that rather than Muslims learning the robustness of the knockabout to-and-fro of public dialogue, we are learning an unnatural and anxious sensitivity. This is reflected in various attempts to curtail freedom of speech such as the (fortunately not wholly successful)

Racial and Religious Hatred Act of 2006. Under the terms of the Bill before it become law, it was quite possible that free interchange with Muslims might have been compromised by a fear that any antagonism arising could have been seen as indicative of an attempt to stir up religious hatred. Subsequent attempts to curb 'extremism' may well present a further threat to free speech.

The very first problem encountered by the young Church is described in detail in Acts chapters 3 and 4. The apostles Peter and John are confronted with the problem of whether they are to obey the command of God or the edicts of the government. They unhesitatingly chose the command of God. We must do the same.

Racism

Not theirs, ours.

There is plenty of racism in Muslim cultures. My valiant efforts to speak Urdu sometimes confuse children, who have very clear ideas concerning who should speak what language. Khalid, a six-year-old, turns to his mother: "Why is this ghora speaking our language?"

"Shush!" she says, and turns red. 'Ghora' a pejorative term for non-Pakistanis, and is pretty well the Urdu equivalent of the slur 'Paki'. He and others could only have learned this at home.

I find this really funny and we have a good laugh; but I do not laugh at my own racism, or temptations to it. If I say that I have conquered all that, I am deluding myself. I need to look at the trigger factors that induce unhealthy feelings of racism or 'culturalism'. These barriers, unless they are exposed and dealt with, lead to hindrances in our relationships. What do I feel when a newly arrived Somali refugee is relentlessly trying to obtain disability benefit on very flimsy grounds? What is my reaction to the NHS spending extra funds on a translator for a lady who has been in Bradford for 20 years but knows no English? These and other 'trigger factors' can set off racist feelings. There are problems; almost certainly they are my problems, but I need to rein in my emotions either way. I need to guard my heart against feelings of outrage and false superiority.

Chapter 7

Open Doors

Education

Burhaan and his wife were wringing their hands. "Why are our kids not like the kids in Pakistan?" said Burhan. "We never expected this...we don't understand them at all!"

Generally speaking, first-generation people of Asian heritage and indigenous British people have little idea what goes on in each other's education systems. Pakistani men such as Burhan, who came to Britain in the 60s to work in factories, went through an Islamic rote education system that has evolved to impart a well-defined body of learning. Concepts such as truth and knowledge are quite rigidly defined and there is no room for questioning or deduction. This start in life did nothing to help Burhan and his generation think or argue constructively, and nor did it give them the tools to adapt to British culture. Their wives may have had no education at all, and many women are illiterate. This means that many Muslim first-generation immigrants in Britain have no way of understanding what is happening to their children, who are going through an entirely different system - one that encourages individual thought and understanding, and where questioning is part of learning.[18]

I am not for a minute saying that British education is perfect. In fact many Muslims are deeply troubled by the secularism of our schools and the divorce between learning and any kind of moral training. The individualism that our education is steeped in has its own problems, and our own culture is as flawed and requires just as much critique as any other. All I am saying is that there are profound differences that make understanding difficult, and which result in young people who go through it turning out very differently.

Burhan and his wife have very little idea of what goes on in a British school. Boys are secure, but girls are often scared that their parents will withdraw them from school if they find out what is going on there. Our own

[18] For a full treatment of the differences between Islamic and British education and the philosophy behind each, please see Caroline Cox and John Marks; *The West, Islam and Islamism* (Civitas, 2003), especially chapter 2, "Concepts of Knowledge and Truth"

daughter went home with a Muslim girl friend who implored her not to talk to her parents about school and in particular not to say that it was mixed. She was frightened that they would discover that the single-sex girls' school where her parents had sent her shared a sixth form with the boy's school nearby, and would withdraw her. In the 1980s and 1990s it was common for girls to be taken out of school when they were about to enter secondary education. They were then sent to Pakistan until they turned sixteen, the school leaving age and the legal age of consent. Then they would return, often to an arranged marriage. Yet girls who escaped this seemed to enjoy school - I recall a stream of intelligent Muslim girls who blossomed at school and developed an acute insight into their own culture. Many of them saw only too clearly how they had been liberated by the very fact that they were being brought up in England, and viewed mainstream state education as their only way out of a kind of cultural imprisonment. They spoke in terms not far removed from panic at the suggestion of Islamic faith schools for Muslim girls. Many young people saw secular state education as the only gap in an increasingly tightly-closed system in which they felt trapped. They wanted to be modern British Asian Muslims; they did not want to be Pakistanis like their parents.

138

Some girls dread being taken out of school prematurely to get married. Afia came into the surgery two days after her sixteenth birthday. She was in tears of rage. "I don't want to be married!" she shouted, banging the table with her hand so forcefully that biros and bits of medical equipment flew into the air. "I don't mind him, he's nice really. But I want to do my A-levels. I want to go to Uni. Why can't I wait?"

Young Muslims educated in Britain are released from the rote system during the daytime but are taught in the mosque after school in the traditional way of their parents. Even now they are likely to be taught by imams who have been brought from Pakistan and who know little English and less of British culture. They teach Islam the way they teach it at home. This means that as far as their religion is concerned young Muslims are still being indoctrinated into a system that does not easily tolerate dissent or discussion. But the effect of the educational difference is to do more than bringing incomprehension and conflict between Muslims educated in Britain and Muslims educated in Pakistan. The rote education system means that people think entirely differently and is a perfect example of a pre-Enlightenment educational worldview. Our way of holding conversations about the Good News is conditioned by the way we ourselves have been educated in a post–Enlightenment environment, and by the similar education of our Western hearers. If Muslim people do not respond to our overtures it is so easy for us to put this rejection down to 'spiritual hardness', when in fact the difficulty is due to our educational differences. If we are to be responsible communicators, we must acknowledge that the fault lies not with them but with us. Muslims will hear the Good News and respond to it in a way that is radically different from the way we do. We are not communicating in a way that they can hear.

One example will serve to illustrate this. When I was a young Christian, people were often urged to "commit your life to Christ". This is not a phrase that is found in the Bible, but God has been very gracious in that it has been very useful in Western culture. The moment we started to talk with Muslims we realised that this phrase was incomprehensible, as was the step by step 'way of salvation'. We had to find another way of expressing the same ideas. Jesus said, "Follow me". This assumes an initial decision to follow and an ongoing resolve to continue following. It is couched in a narrative about walking along the beach, about fishing boats and nets, and at once conjures up a picture in the mind's eye. There are very few cultures where this does not conjure up some kind of mental image. It may need to be carefully worked out, but it's initial meaning is immediately accessible. This metaphor crosses cultural and educational divides.

Western education does not by itself solve the 'one word, two meanings' problem. That problem is ours to solve. But Muslims, especially women, who receive a Western education, are liberated from an environment in which they can speak only their mother tongue. It enables them to think for themselves rather than being locked into a traditional system where what is taught is held to be correct without question. More, it enables men and especially women to develop a sense of personal identity, rather than a sense of role. For a young woman in a Pakistani family in Punjab it is unthinkable that she might make a decision about her own life. Such decisions are made corporately with older people, not on an individual basis. Even in England the idea of privacy and personal autonomy is not well-developed in many Muslim families.

Of course the cult of the individual brings with it huge problems, but the fact remains that Western and British educational approaches release young Muslim people from the traditional constraints of their parents' generation, allowing them to consider the Gospel of Christ with a far greater degree of freedom.

Spoken language

Western education does something even more important; it teaches Muslims to speak English (or French or any other European language) so that they are effectively bilingual. This means that for the first time in history we in the West have an effective means of communication without needing to become experts in a foreign language. We can talk of 'heart' and 'gut' matters as well as 'head' matters with our Muslim friends. Throughout the history of Christian mission, Islam has been regarded as difficult and problematic, an area where special training and dedication is required. To a large extent this is because of language problems. At a stroke this barrier is removed.

The cringe factor

What do nearly all people in Britain feel when they sense that you are about to open a conversation about something personal and serious? They cringe! There is an immediate air of tension. You are labelled as a Bible-basher, one of those well-meaning and earnest people who are going to corner you for your own good. This 'cringe factor' is a person's greatest defence against hearing the vital news about Christ. Anyone who wants to open a conversation about God with a friend must first gain his or her confidence, and persuade them that they are not in for a time of excruciating embarrassment.

It is the most wonderful thing to discover that this 'cringe factor' is entirely absent amongst Muslims, who are used to talking about Islam very naturally all the time. I find that in the course of my work as a GP, matters of faith are brought up in a very natural and unselfconscious way. I can offer to pray with people far more freely than I can with secular people.

This is not a sign of spiritual openness. Even a person who does not want to talk about spiritual things is in no way put out by the suggestion; it is entirely cultural, but it is extraordinarily liberating, and it means that we must discard the tension and embarrassment that might have been the habit of a lifetime when we start to talk with Muslim people about the Good News.

Visiting

Another very liberating aspect of Muslim cultures is the visit. In British culture I have to be invited to someone's home and there is a diary consultation to arrange a time. If someone comes to our house uninvited there is one question that is uppermost: what is the visit for? What is the agenda? In fact it is very hard for me to visit a British person's home without a pretext. How strange it would be if a person who is not a very special friend or a relative came and went without a reason; you would find yourself saying, "So why did they come?"

In Muslim cultures, on the other hand, there need be no reason whatever. If you go to someone's house then it is 'a visit' and no one will ask why you have come or even think it. It is just a visit. This again is liberating. If you have made an acquaintance and feel that this could blossom into a friendship, then...visit! You don't have to think up an excuse. However I often ask Muslim men if I might visit, and I always get a very welcoming response. I know that this is genuine because hospitality is so deeply rooted in virtually all Muslim cultures. Across all the rich variety of Muslim civilisation this seems remarkably consistent.

So when you arrive at your friend's home, what happens?

Firstly you will be aware that this is not just 'getting to know you'. As this is your first visit you are there to honour your friend's family and his home. It will be good if you take your whole family if you have one: if you are single then take a friend or two. Do not go empty handed; a large box of chocolates or sweets is a very suitable present. Dress up!

As you go in there will be a pile of shoes on the floor somewhere and this is where you take off your own. Even if your host tells you not to bother, you must take your shoes off. Nearly all Muslim homes have a guest room where you will be ushered and no expense will have been spared to make it impressive and showy. Even in modest homes there will be plush armchairs, perhaps in deep red velvet. This is not for show; this is a very important room where guests are honoured.

Once you are settled, the ladies may be swept off to the ladies quarters. The children will also disappear to reappear later, the girls with their fingernails painted and dressed in clothing that definitely is not theirs. Your hosts may be mystified that your little girl of five hasn't even had her ears pierced. Children are the most wonderful cross-cultural workers, breaking down barriers that otherwise take months or years to overcome.

You will be offered tea or coffee, and in England you will be asked to choose between "English or like we do it". Always choose their way. You will be offered food. Always accept and eat it with obvious enjoyment. This is never a hardship as food in Muslim homes is invariably delicious and far superior to any restaurant from the same culture. Warn the children that they must eat what is put in front of them. Any complaints can be heard only when you are safely back home! Your host may leave the room when you are eating, or for that matter at any time. This will seem strange at first, as in Western culture it is most impolite to leave one's guests, but in most Islamic cultures it is perfectly normal.

Future visits are much more relaxed, but you must still be careful to honour the home by taking off your shoes and staying in the guest room until invited elsewhere.

And finally...

Many Muslims are liberated to a large extent by education, speak English naturally, and are politically free to hear the Gospel. They are also on our doorstep. This means that we as Christians do not have to spend long years training in areas of expertise like our predecessors, such as Raymond Lull, Henry Martyn, William Temple Gairdner and others. Nor do we need the expensive paraphernalia of a mission society to support us in a distant country. However, we do need to understand that we frequently speak a different language than our Muslim friends, even though we use the same words. God has brought many Muslims close to us because he wants to bless them. He wants them to come to know and love his son, Jesus Christ.

Chapter 8

Being There, Saying It

Being

To share the Good News with Muslim men and women we must *be there* with them. But first, before we can be there, we must first of all *be*.

We no longer have to be experts, as we will be seeing later in this chapter, but what then must we be?

Firstly, we must be serious and enthusiastic Christian men and women, filled with the Holy Spirit and with love.

"He who believes in me, out of his heart shall flow rivers of living water." (John ch. 7 v.38)

Do we take this verse seriously? Do we have the living water that will overflow? We can speak about Jesus in words, and the words will be true; but they may nevertheless be empty. We use the phrase "sharing the Gospel" and how true! The Gospel can only be shared;

we can only give what we already have. The only bread that I can offer is the bread that I hold in my hand.

I know the words. These words are readily available. I can preach them from my head, and I understand what they mean. But we have already seen that the head is not the place where the love and the power exist. Theology is immensely important, but I cannot stop there; for me to offer a living reality about God I must first know it, know its power, its joy, its pain, its severity. I must have, in some tiny way, experienced Christ; I must know something of the awesome character of God and the terribleness of his hatred of everything that is wrong; I must have been astonished and overwhelmed at the marvel of his love for me and the extraordinary depth of his goodness to me. I must look back and see where I have come from, my dire need of rescue, the pitiful state of hopelessness and alienation that he drew me from; and I must look to the present, to the status that God has given me in his Son. That I should have a place with him in his heavenly kingdom - that I should be called his child, and inherit all the rights and delights of his home - I must find it a ceaseless wonder that God should have chosen me and overwhelmed me with good things and that this fierce and profligate God should have treated me according to his own holy character, and not according to my own.

And I must be sure that Islam can provide none of these things. I have known and loved many Muslims, some of them deeply devout, some very secular, at least on the surface, and some for whom their religion sits lightly on their shoulders. I have never ceased to mourn at the poverty of their faith - the religiousness that soothes but never satisfies the deep cravings of the heart or the hunger for forgiveness and love.

What do I want for my hungry Muslim friends? I want all that I myself have received. I do not want to share an anaemic faith that has neither power nor attraction. I want to share my knowledge of a God who is real, strong, loving, sometimes fierce, dangerous - and fun! To do this I must know him. I must be an apprentice, a servant and child of Jesus.

Saying it - your Christian story

The disciple who wants to point the way to Jesus must be able to articulate some of this. This is what Christians call 'testimony'. It is being able to talk to your Muslim friend about your experience of God. After all, God is not only a God who speaks but a God who acts: he is a God who does things.

This is not a concept that features strongly in the mindset of most Muslims. God has spoken. He is a lawgiver. There is a past in which God created the world, created man, and had men who followed him and were good Muslims. There is a future, in that there is a judgement day, and there is reward and punishment in the afterlife, but God is not seen to act directly in the lives of people in the present moment. Perhaps this is because events are mactoob; they are 'written down', and in consequence, unchangeable. Though there are certainly Muslim men and women who feel that they can pray to God directly and that he hears them, this idea of the fixity of the future, the fatalistic idea that 'what will be is God's will', is deeply ingrained in the Muslim mindset, and militates against the idea not only of answered prayer but also of a person having direct experiences of God or a relationship with him. That is why it is so important to tell your story; it is a way of saying "But God isn't like that!"

Another concept we have mentioned earlier excludes relationship; the monolithic and repeatedly stressed oneness of God. In mainstream Islam (but not among all), the idea of a relationship as Christians understand it is nonexistent. The way people relate to God is through 'religion', and, as we have seen, Islam's self-view is very much as a religion. The Muslim pattern is that men and women exist as slaves of God. Hence the many Muslim names such as Abdulla (slave of God), Abdul Raheem (slave of the merciful), and Abdul Karim (slave of the generous).

It is here that the Christian and the Muslim concept of God are at their most divergent. As I have said earlier, Christianity's view of itself is not as religion but as relationship. God expresses perfectly his relational character in the Trinity, and God's perfect expression of himself in human terms is in his Son: "...in Christ all the fullness of the Deity lives in bodily form" (Col. ch.2 v.9). Jesus tells God's children to address God as Father. We are in Christ, as Christ is in the Father (John ch.17 v.21). Paul's letter to the Colossians unfolds our status in Christ: as his people we are holy and dearly loved (Col. ch.3 v.12); we are reconciled former enemies, holy, without blemish and free from accusation (Col. ch.1 v.22). We have been given fullness in Christ who himself is the fullness of God in bodily form (Col. ch..2 v.9), and every bit of it is absolutely conditional on Christ and the very presence of the Holy Spirit.

You are speaking of what God has done; how he has answered prayer, led you, brought you to himself. These parts of your story are all immensely important. And not only the high points, the disappointments too! You may think these experiences are dull and uninteresting; let your Muslim friend be the judge of that. You are likely to find that they are anything but dull to him or her. By telling your own story you are stressing the difference between their God and yours, but without rubbing it in. Your experience of God cuts across their picture of God as essentially inactive when it comes to our tiny individual lives, and is all the more arresting and powerful for that. It makes any Gospel talk you may do jump out of the pages of a book written long ago and into the present moment.

But your story is more important than that. God's dealings with you are, in a tiny and mysterious way, in continuity with his dealings with the people of the Bible. God's way is the way of history. The Jews told and retold to themselves again and again the story of God's intervention in their lives - his rescue, his providence, his love and concern, his revelation of his own holy character, his discipline and chastisement when they went off the rails. Prophets reminded the people. Praying men and women 'reminded' God. Our experience with him is a tiny reflection of this. God has a grand narrative and a plan, and the Good News of Christ is expressed in real events in real time. We and our own story are part of this. To recall some of this story is a blessing to ourselves as well as to others, and it brings glory to God.

If you have known God only a short time, the way you became a Christian might be sharply etched in your recent memory, and be the experience you would like to talk about most. If you have spent a lifetime as a Christian, there will be in your consciousness a sense of a life spent with God.

There will be things of an intensely private nature: inner battles fought over many years, often lost, sometimes won - sins battled with, shame overcome. These are private things and it may be quite wrong to share them. There are secret things between you and God that should remain secret.

But there are things that bless others in the telling. God's provision in times of need; his tenderness and presence in trouble and adversity. How he has helped in bringing up children. How things were difficult, how you messed up; how sometimes you felt his absence keenly just when you wanted him to be there.

And then there is how God has acted not only with you as an individual, but how he has worked in you and others as part of a team in his service. In southern Sudan in the early 1980s my wife and I were members of a group of missions and agencies doing relief and development work. In our headquarters we did not have a very high view of ourselves as a Christian fellowship and were prone to introspection as to why our relationships were so mediocre. Then out of the blue six members of our team were taken hostage by a screaming mad revolutionary and his guerrilla army. We feared for their lives moment by moment, and negotiations (taking place by radio) were on a perpetual knife-edge. Prayer was offered constantly, and in a fortnight the situation was successfully resolved, unbelievably without a drop of blood shed.

Some Americans from the CIA were parachuted in. When it was all over one of them asked me to take him to Konya Konya, a well known colourful market full of stalls that sold handmade produce, from brass bracelets to shoes made from old car tyres, so that he could buy his wife some souvenirs.

Hardly had we left the guest house when he rounded on me. "What is it with you people?" he said, stabbing his finger into my chest. "I've been to dozens of kidnappings; the rule is that the organisation is blown to bits. People just don't cope and the set-up disintegrates. That's the way it always is. But you lot...look at you...you just go on; you hold together; you even pray for your enemies!"

He was determined to know the secret. He and his team had lived with us for a fortnight and had seen our faith - for what it was worth. He was deeply challenged and unsettled by a response that he had never encountered to a kind of trauma in which he was very experienced.

The answer? God was at work in our mediocre little fellowship and we never saw it until that moment! Here was a testimony more powerful than any individual story. And his response was a blessing to us, as our own perspective was that we were very ordinary and had only struggled on as best we could. It did not occur to us that there was anything special going on. Your story depends on reality and truth and the underlying hopes and expectations of God that are revealed in an ordinary story far more than in any drama. Nevertheless your witness to your experience of God can be humorous - and fun!

And as well as *saying it*, we must *be there*.

Being There: a story in two chapters

Chapter One: There was once a country called Roundia. It was called that because it was round and comfortable, like a jam doughnut. And all the people in Roundia were happy with its shape. Roundia had many Christians, and many strong Christian churches.

A long way away there was a square country - called, naturally enough, Squaria. One day the Christians in Roundia looked across at Squaria and, hard as they looked, they could see no Christians. They at once called a meeting and discussed what they should do. After a while they decided that they should go and tell the Squarians about Jesus and his love for them. They set up a sub-committee to look into this and to arrange it.

The sub-committee soon found that there were a lot of difficulties in the way of this plan. For a start the Squarians spoke a language that no one could understand, and had a culture that seemed inscrutable. The Squarian government was very hostile to any idea of people talking about Jesus, and tended to throw people into prison if they did. They had secret police and the country was hot and full of both frightening insects and strange diseases. Squaria was a long way away and it was expensive to get there and live there. And there were no schools where the Roundians could educate their children.

After much work, the churches trained people in the language and culture of Squaria. After some time these people left Roundia and arrived in Squaria. They became expert in dealing with the government, survived (mostly) the heat, the insects and the diseases, and they talked about the Good News of Jesus. These people the church called 'missionaries'. They were regarded as a little bit special, which was not surprising considering the hurdles that they had to overcome to get their work done.

By the grace of God, some Squarians became Christians, and churches were established.

Chapter Two: One morning the Roundians woke up and, looking out of their bedroom windows, found that the shape of their country had changed. Instead of the comfortable round doughnut shape that they knew and loved, their country had a huge hole in the middle; it had become like a bagel. Looking a second time they saw that something else had happened too: the big hole in the middle was full of Squarians!

The Christians held another meeting. One person after another spoke in excited terms. "God has brought the Squarians onto our very doorsteps!" they exclaimed; "We must send missionaries to the Squarians in our midst!"

"Look!", said one man, "It costs us an arm and a leg to send people to Squaria, but now I can get to the Squarians on the No. 36 bus!"

"Yes," said a lady, "and some of them speak English very well, so well we can really communicate."

"And," exclaimed a third, "all those rules about 'preaching the Good News' we had to be so careful about - we can really talk about Jesus freely now because this is our own country!"

They were about to vote on the 'sending missionaries' motion when, at the back of the hall, a very old man stood up.

"No!", he shouted, waving his stick, "we should not be sending missionaries!"

There was a stunned and uncomprehending silence.

"No!", he said again, even more emphatically.

"But whyever not?", the people asked.

"We have just heard a lot of people telling us why missionaries are not needed," said the old man. "The Squarians are down the road instead of thousands of miles away. They speak English well. We have freedom to work among them, to make friends and to get to know them, and to talk about the Good News with them. No, we should not send missionaries. We should not send anybody. We should all go."

This little story simplifies and overstates, but nevertheless illustrates something important. There has been a 'missionary' paradigm that has been useful, and not altogether unscriptural (although it ignores the many other ways that God uses to spread the Good News apart from 'missionaries'). Very committed people have spent many years training and enduring enormous difficulties so that they can share God's message with those in strange and difficult countries; and they still do. I don't for a minute wish to denigrate these people. A central part of the work of the Church is to do precisely this - to send people to countries where there are no Christians and no churches. This work has its own excitements and pleasures, but these people frequently endure danger and live mostly in obscurity and with little money. Sometimes the results are spectacular but it is often many years before they see any results for their work, and sometimes there are no results at all in their own lifetimes. There are many Christians from all over the world living and working in a huge variety of situations, and this is absolutely necessary - it is our answer to the central call of Jesus, who told us to "Go into all the world". The danger is that this paradigm remains in the minds of churches and church leaders when and where the conditions that gave rise to it have radically altered.

In the last chapter we saw how, like in the story, huge barriers have been removed, vast distances reduced to a bus ride, language barriers overcome, costs reduced to insignificance, political barriers made non-existent. While other problems remain, the old man was right to see that the specialist 'missionary' is not required, and that the concept gets in the way of the church's work, as church members feel excluded from getting involved because they do not have the necessary expertise. Of course, men and women with cross-cultural and other skills and experience are hugely helpful, but their absence should not deter 'ordinary' church members from getting stuck in. There are wonderful things happening amongst and through people who have no 'expertise' whatsoever!

The Roundia-Squaria picture is exactly that in British cities like London, Birmingham and Sheffield. There are strong churches (the Roundians) on the periphery of towns, and very weak (in terms of numbers) churches in the centre, where the newly-arrived (the Squarians) are to be found. An additional problem is that all too often, people worship in an inner-city church even though they have long since left the area for a house in a more up-market area, so even the number of worshippers is a misleading indication of how many Christians are actually living or working there. Often the big churches are committed to supporting 'missionary work' abroad, and look at the newly-arrived in their own cities in the same way. The right response to the wide-open opportunity on our doorsteps is not to send a select few, but for many to go; to establish churches with significant numbers of church members who will not bus in from outside but who will devote a realistic part of their time and energy to the place where they also worship.

Of course it is far from being that simple. It is a big step for those with little cross-cultural experience or inclination to go down to the areas where all the faces look foreign, the clothing is all alien, and the signs on the shops are in a strange script - but hey, its not really that strange, you'll soon get used to it, and you will end up really enjoying it! It just needs a friend who is familiar with the environment to take you round, to visit a few homes and find that the people in these shops and homes are real live breathing people who are not entirely unlike you.

This represents a major challenge to our Christian commitment. The communities in our inner cities that originate from overseas, although very much more accessible than their home communities, are still very alien to those of us who come from leafy suburbs or expensive town houses. But what about all those phrases that trip off the tongue about 'giving all to Christ'? "You will be my witnesses," Jesus said, and went on, "in Judaea, Samaria and the uttermost parts of the world".

The uttermost parts of the world? Yes, but how about Samaria, only a bus ride away?

The Son of Man *came*. Jesus himself came into the world. It is that simple. Where would we be if he had not? But that is not his character - to stay where he was, in safety, comfort and glory. His character is to take on the form of a servant, to eat with reprobates and outcasts, to get his feet first dirty and eventually covered in blood. To wash the feet of his followers, to go without sleep and without food, to share his very self with the ones he loved. This is not merely what he did, it is who he is.

In practical terms, how do we do this? The many Muslim areas in our country are in fact easily entered if we use a little imagination and a little courage. We looked at this earlier; there are dozens of jobs that require workers to visit homes. A video repair man knew many families in the area I once worked. Health visitors, plumbers, delivery men, dustbin men, council workers, garage mechanics and a host of others all do work that can lead to rewarding relationships. School teachers and classroom assistants in particular are much valued by children and teenagers in Muslim areas, as they form a contact outside their own culture when so many feel 'locked in'. There is no skill or trade that is useless to God in his pursuit of those he to whom he wishes to show his love. And then there is the enormous and varied voluntary sector. With such variety, there is something to suit every taste and talent.

The church that we belonged to had a unique feature; many - or all - of the local churches consisted of members who had moved out of town as the area had become increasingly Asian, and commuted in weekly for their services in the way I outlined earlier. They had abandoned the locale in every respect save that it was still their geographical place of worship. However, our own church had a number of families who had bought homes in the neighbourhood and were living among Muslims. It was often not an easy existence, but it was one that led to naturally maturing relationships with their neighbours and a relaxed witness from people who were part of the furniture.

These families had a profound effect on the whole church, and gave purpose to its existence. There was a deep sense of having a calling to the people of the area.

How did the church and our work in the surgery connect? We could not point to any kind of organic or organisational unity. Some in the church had other interests, some we hardly knew, some of our team belonged to others than the messy, international bunch that was our own church; but the overriding feeling was that we are part of the church. We were just all there.

Our own move into a Muslim area had very clear aims. We wanted to work as a Christian team and not as individuals, and we wanted to meet a great many people in a relaxed and natural way, and in a situation where they could be free of the constraints of their own culture. We wanted to put the skills we had at God's service. We wanted to see and demonstrate the love and power of God before thinking of 'evangelism', and we wanted to be linked intimately with a church that had the same kind of outlook. It seemed that a medical general practice surgery was not such a bad idea.

Fully part of the NHS General Practice system, our surgery was free to adopt the character its workers felt appropriate as long as the 'Terms of Service' - the kind of service that under the National Health Service we were contracted to provide - were adhered to. In those days, the end of the 1980s and early 90s, these were very flexible, and in many ways still are. This gave us the opportunity to develop a team that was Christian at the core but could never become a 'holy huddle' as so many other health service people worked with us on a daily basis. People of all races, and of all faiths (and none) came in and out of our working environment. There was no pretending. People saw us as we were.

One evening, leaving work after a more than usually gruelling surgery, I stood with my hand on the car door. I was snowed under. I could not cope with anything more. I knew that there were many drug addicts and numbers of prostitutes out there in the neighbourhood. It was just that we had not encountered them. I said a silent prayer of gratitude that God had not called us to work with these people.

A week or so later The Captain sat in the waiting room. Small and thin, Ameed seemed far from military. Ameed wanted help coming off heroin. What were we going to do to help him?

Ameed's friends were not far behind him. Within a few weeks we were involved with a small but demanding group, nearly all of Pakistani origin. It fitted ill with our normal family clientele, but these young men, and the few women, showed an extraordinary spiritual hunger.

"When do you have your meeting?" said one of the street girls to my wife.

There was no meeting.

"Thursday evenings," she said promptly, and that was how our Thursday evening meetings started, an odd mixture of Christian songs, prayer, Bible discussion and writing methadone prescriptions. There was an extraordinary sense of worship among the dozen or so men and women there. "I have never worshipped God until now," said Karim, one of our heroin addicts.

A group of volunteers came together. Colin came from a well-established Christian drug rescue initiative, and others came to spend evenings or weekends with our friends as we stood by them as they 'did turkey'. We found that praying and singing with them meant that the dreaded symptoms of withdrawal just never appeared. The Captain, who had 'turkeyed' in police cells on at least two occasions, could not believe what was happening to him. "Why am I not rattling?" he kept saying.

We rented a large house near the surgery and Colin looked after a group of men who had succeeded in coming off heroin. We all pitched in and helped. We went to court with our friends when the police caught up with them, and visited them in prison. There was a team from different churches that acted in concert in this exhausting work. Here was the body of Christ in action. It was 'being there'.

But there was another dimension that took us beyond the team, and that was family. We had four teenagers living in our home, preoccupied with school, growing up, sport, puberty, homework, music, relationships. Into this came Muslim friends, drug addicts and the occasional prostitute. All were treated to our 'open home' environment. There was no pretence here either. Our non-Christian friends were exposed to the unexpurgated reality of a 'Christian' home, with all its warts and imperfections. We would sit for hours over the dinner table battling with the questions of life, death, politics, everything. Anyone who was there joined in. The other families in the practice were alike, though far more recently married and with much younger children, if any. This meant that we were not just one-dimensional 'professionals'

Two young Muslim drug addicts came to church every Sunday. Afterwards they came to our house, where they ate and talked. We provided a place for Wakeel to meet his girlfriend in a secure and wholesome environment. 'Fundamentalists' came to cross swords with us.

Enquiring minds and hearts came to think, talk and listen. It was all very exciting, and very exhausting.

Chapter 9

Praying

I was attending a small church seminar one Saturday morning. The speaker was a short fiery Indian whose name, to my great regret, I have forgotten. At lunchtime a few of us went out to buy some chips. He turned to me. "Do you pray with your patients?" he said.

"I can go home now," I thought, (though I stayed). I felt God had spoken to me with absolute clarity, and I will always be grateful to my unknown Indian friend. It was in this way that we started to incorporate prayer for people into the ordinary life and work of the surgery.

A week or two later I was still wondering how to get going. Farida, an overweight and surly 16-year-old, came to the surgery. Having recently completed a full course of treatment for TB of the spine, she had made a full recovery but had been told that the damage done would result in permanent backache. It explained her grumpy mood.

She suddenly asked: "If you pray for my back, will it get better?" I thought, with most uncharacteristic logic and speed, that there were three answers to that question: 'yes', 'no' and 'maybe'. 'Maybe' was by far the safest, but was a cop-out. Besides, I was then only offering her what she could get in Islam, where 'Inshaa'Allah' was a safe and very common expression meaning 'if God wills it'. Surely as a Christian I could offer her more hope than that - and 'no' was obviously out of the question. Which left only 'yes'.

"Yes," I said.

"Pray then," she said rather abruptly. I said a very brief, one-sentence prayer. As she got up to leave her eyes filled with tears. "And will you pray for me to get pregnant please? I've been married for six months; my mother-in-law has gone to Pakistan. She told me. 'you be pregnant my girl, by the time I get back, or you're for it'".

Feeling that things were getting out of control I asked the lady who cleaned the surgery for us to come in and pray. Our prayer was as brief and perfunctory as the first. Farida left. We got on with the surgery.

There were more tears only a week or two later. Rahma, a 26-year-old from a Ugandan Asian family, came to us in great distress. She had had no less than five miscarriages. Apart from the repeated shock and distress these had caused, she was under severe pressure from the family to produce a child. We discussed the issues: there is little that one can do ahead of time in these circumstances, and in the 1990s there was even less. I promised to refer her to the hospital the moment she came up with a positive pregnancy test.

It was only a few weeks later that the phone woke me at 2am. Rahma was pregnant and bleeding, She was on the way to her sixth miscarriage. Half asleep, I pulled on my clothes. When I arrived, there was Rahma in bed surrounded by half a dozen ladies sitting round the room.

It was clear that Rahma was losing the baby. I looked at the rather terrifying squad of ladies. "Rahma is going to lose this baby," I said, but would you like me to ask God to do something?" There were silent nods. "I am going to ask in Jesus name," I went on, "Jesus has the miracles. Is that okay?" More nods.

I prayed very briefly in Jesus name. We talked a little, and I left for home. I rang the next day. The bleeding had stopped. I held my breath.

Rahma continued with a normal pregnancy and produced a lovely little girl.

Several weeks later Farida came for another matter. "About my back Doc," she said casually, "its completely better!"

I next saw her much later when she was about seven months pregnant. I could see immediately that something was wrong. "Remember you prayed for me to get pregnant Doc?" she said, "Well, I've been fine but I haven't felt the baby kick since yesterday."

I listened for her baby's heartbeat. I listened hard in many different places. I heard nothing.

"It's okay, isn't it?" she said anxiously.

It was one of those moments when I felt that God was either there or he wasn't and if he wasn't we had better find out quickly. And if he was, let's go for it! If God had started something here, he would finish it. Feeling as though I was in freefall I said. "I'm going to send you up for a scan at the hospital, but the baby's okay."

Later that evening she rang me. "Just wanted to let you know that everything's fine, Doc," she said cheerfully, and rang off.

We had more answers to prayers that were often nothing to do with medical matters. Ibrahim was a middle-aged Yemeni man whose wife was still in

Yemen; he had been trying for years to obtain a visa for her. After we prayed for Ibrahim his wife was in England within the month.

Occasionally people would take the initiative and ask for prayer: a good friend, Omar, who I have already mentioned, lived over the road from the surgery. We had enjoyed some times of reading the Bible, he just loved to talk about Jesus, and he clearly had a lively faith that was just about tolerated by his wife Sultana, a strong Muslim. One day he came to the surgery with what was clearly an unpleasant attack of bronchitis. Relieved at what was essentially an uncomplicated consultation I gave him a course of antibiotics.

Two days later Sultana came by. "How is Omar, is he better?" I asked.

"Of course he isn't better!" she said crossly; "How could he be better? You didn't even pray for him!" Mortified, I went to see him later that morning and we prayed together. He recovered well.

A young man rushed in one day, greatly agitated. "My mother in Pakistan is really sick," he said, "I'm going tonight; will you pray for her?" Taken aback and full of the business of the evening surgery, I said a short prayer. "Thanks Doc!" he said, and rushed out as quickly as he had come. Back at work, I quickly forgot all about the incident. A few weeks later the same young man came again. "Doc," he shouted, "Mum is well. God has answered! She got better really quick; thanks!"

Did we pray for everyone? No; there were many days and sometimes weeks when we prayed for nobody. We just seemed to work, and go home exhausted. Other members of our surgery team prayed for many whom they came into contact with, and as often as we could we asked one or more members of the team to pray with us, but very often the demands of work meant that there was no one available, or that there simply wasn't the time. There were always many people to see and too little time to see them.

We had always started work with prayer - there was a fifteen-minute slot at the beginning of the day when all six or so staff gathered together to pray. On Thursdays we started an hour late and spent the first hour praying and praising God. Most of the team were there and there were also a few friends who made it a priority to come along on Thursday mornings. We would look up and see noses pressed to the window. People were aware that we prayed and somehow appreciated it. It rapidly became impossible to start work without prayer; those few minutes in the morning became an indispensible part of our working life.

Did God always answer our prayers? No; there were times when nothing seemed to happen, or we just never really found out what had happened. But it seems that every time we asked God to intervene - or our patients asked us to ask - something happened in our relationship with the people concerned. Many years after leaving the area I saw Rafiq sitting on a wall and we got chatting. "You prayed for my dad," he said, matter-of-factly. This was perhaps twelve years previously, and I had rather uncomfortable memories of the event. Rafiq's father had suffered from a lymphoma which I had been rather slow to detect. No harm had come of the delay and he had made a complete recovery, but I was very aware that I should have moved faster. Rafiq chose not to mention this; instead simply mentioning that we had prayed for his father.

What became rapidly clear was that people loved to be prayed for. There was none of the embarrassment that might have been felt with secular people. We would of course offer prayer in a very tactful way, with plenty of 'let outs', though in practice people very seldom if ever used the escape routes that we offered. We would make it clear then that we were going to pray in the name of

Jesus, "because Jesus has the power to heal," or if it was not a matter of healing, because Jesus has power over the Housing Department or the Foreign Office. There would be a stock response to this: people would usually say, "oh yes, we love Jesus too; we believe he is a prophet." We would let this pass; this was not a time for a discussion, it was a time for prayer. I remember only one man ever changing his mind after realising that we were going to pray in Jesus name, but if someone was a little hesitant it was very easy to say "okay, let's just leave it till another time." Recently while I was working in a practice in the north of England a lady came with her mother and said rather suddenly, "I want you to pray for me." I was taken aback. Only later did I remember that I had suggested weeks previously that we mention her problem to God. Seeing that she was a little hesitant I had quickly suggested we leave it, saying she could always ask at some future time. She did!

Of course we never used the word 'prayer', preferring to 'ask God to do something', or to 'ask God to make you better'. 'Prayer' is a word used a great deal in the Muslim world, and we did not want to confuse matters. What we wanted to communicate was that God was interested in them personally, and that he was interested enough - and close enough - to intervene directly in their daily lives; in fact far more than this, that he actually loved them and wanted them to come to know him.

Prayer is a wonderful way of communicating the love of God. An awareness of our wrong-doing and God's judgement is a very serious and essential part of the Good News, yet we felt nearly all the time that the good news of God's love for the people we were speaking to was something overriding that we needed to share. They knew much about God's fierceness, his power, and his judgement. They knew little or nothing of his love.

A rather more hidden - but important - agenda was to show how different the God of Islam and the God of Christianity actually were. As I mentioned in the last chapter, the God of Islam says a lot but does little; that is why so many Muslims take recourse to magic and the occult. We would always in our prayers address God as Father; no Muslim calls God 'Father', and this at once accentuates the difference. Besides, he actually is our father! Our Father delights to hear the prayers of his children, especially for those who do not know him and to whom he wants to show himself. Actually we modelled this kind of prayer on what Jesus did in the course of his life. Even when we allow for an abbreviated narrative, we can see in the Bible that his encounters with people were very short. In a moment they experienced his power to heal or deliver, with no religious add-ons.

And what were our prayers like? They were simple and short to the point of banality. What would we say? An example would be, "Father, I ask in Jesus name that you will make Ahmed's leg pain better...amen."

"Father, thank you that Issa the Messiah has the miracles and can bring down little Aisha's fever. Please do it Lord, in Issa Massih's name, amen"

"Father, you have heard us talking about the fighting in Jamil's street and the trouble between the families. Please bring peace to their street, in Jesus' name, amen."

We used words that were brief, simple and ordinary. There were no religious words or religious overtones; we were in a busy marketplace with people who knew no Christian jargon. Even when we were in people's homes, prayer was short. People would look up and say "Is that it?" "Yes!" I would say, telling them that this was a word to our father directly, and definitely not a religious or magic formula.

And sometimes people would look up and say, "and Doc, while we are at it, would you pray for...." and bring up someone or something that was troubling them, and we would pray again. It seemed special when we were actually asked to pray.

Prayer jumps the Christian-Muslim divide in a single leap. Prayer invites God to act and speak to people who do not know Jesus in a language they understand. Even when God does little in practical terms, the relationship is subtly changed, and sometimes transformed. But prayer is also a way in which we ourselves discover if God is actually there. This can be truly terrifying. After many years of praying for people I am convinced that God is really there, and that he is not inactive or uninterested in ordinary men and women. Moreover, God delights to answer prayer for those who do not yet know him. "I seem to have a one hundred percent success rate when it comes to praying for Muslims!" said a family doctor friend, and I have heard the same story from others.

Jesus infuriated his hearers at Nazareth when he told them that during the famine in Elijah's time there were many hungry people in Israel but God met the needs of one person - an unbelieving gentile. There were many lepers in Israel in Elisha's time but again, God healed only one - another unbelieving gentile. Most, perhaps all of Jesus' miracles happened to people who were not

'Christians'. Could it be true that Jesus' healing is mostly, for people who do not know him?

Prayer depends too on the extraordinary generosity of God. At the wedding in Cana, Jesus created a huge surplus of wine for those who had already drunk more than enough. He did the same when he fed the five thousand, producing a bread mountain that filled twelve baskets. The Prodigal Son returns to a father's welcome that, by all reasonable standards, is completely over the top. Jesus shows us something special about God's character; that he is wildly generous, to the point of profligacy. How could it be otherwise when he has given us everything that he has in the shape of his one and only son?

Finally, prayer depends on Jesus' accessibility. Where are the great intercessors of the New Testament? It may take a moment to locate them as they are so invisible. What is an intercessor? Someone who approaches God on behalf of someone else with a determination to get what they want!

The centurion forgets his position in order to intercede for his servant and Jesus is amazed at his faith (Matthew ch.8 v.5). The four men are so determined to get their paralysed friend to where Jesus could see him that they are prepared to climb onto the roof and do material damage to what might have been Jesus' own house (Luke ch.5 v.17). A Samaritan woman is so determined to get Jesus' attention that she is prepared to be ignored and insulted (Matthew ch.15 v.21). A deaf man is brought by 'some people' and is healed (Mark ch.7 v.32). These people are so obscure that that they have no names - and yet without them the servant, the paralysed man, and the deaf mute would never have been healed. They were the intercessors of the day.

Either Jesus is the same, yesterday, today and forever, or his he not. If he is, then we can bring others to him in the same way as did those nameless intercessors whose faith Jesus praised. A friend tells me of a group of women who were praying for a Muslim lady who had breast cancer. The lady was completely healed. These women are as unknown as the men who brought the deaf mute to Jesus. He heard their prayer and healed their friend. It is a thrill to be reminded that God is at work in the same way today.

"You prayed, and God did not answer! Where is your God now?" is the inevitable question. I have been waiting for this - and I have never heard it from anyone. I have only ever heard it in my own thoughts. A couple of Sudanese friends prayed for a very sick little girl, the daughter of Sudanese nomads, in Port Sudan. They had been reading the Bible together with the family for months, and they had a lovely relationship. Now the little girl was very sick. "Surely God must answer," I thought, "it is so strategic, - here are southern Sudanese Christians meeting with a nomadic tribe among whom there are almost no known believers. Surely God will heal her, and show this family that he is really there?"

God looked at things differently. The little girl did not get better. She died.

I was upset and angry. "Where are you for these people, God?" I shouted inside. It seems as though I was the only one who did. Her family and friends wept and buried their little girl in a country where many suffer and many little children die. The friendship between the families continued; the Bible and its message continued to be read and shared.

Prayer requires no special 'gift', and it requires no special training. It needs only a desire to see God actually do things for people, and a little faith - like a tiny mustard seed - that he will act. I never expect people who are not Christians to have faith - but amazingly, they often do. Having faith is the job of those of us who in some small way have known God. It is the job of the people who bring people to Jesus like the nameless men and women I have mentioned earlier, and it is for the Christian. But often Muslims have faith in Issa too.

In the Sudanese church no one would dream of leaving the house of a sick person without prayer. We found that this was a good habit. Prayer is what Christian people do.

Chapter 10

The Bible

As a hard-working language student in Jordan I was keen to use my regular half an hour's taxi ride to good effect. Opening my Arabic New Testament I began to plod through the day's lesson as we crashed over the Amman potholes. How would my fellow travellers react? Would they be offended that here in a Muslim country this foreigner next to them was flagrantly reading a Bible?

I was unprepared for what happened next. The two men either side of me were immediately curious and both of them started reading over my shoulder. When I started to turn the page one said, "hang on, I haven't finished yet!" One was reading almost audibly. In a few moments a discussion had begun.

I was having a rapid induction into the way Muslim people - at least, the ones I have come across - look at the Bible. I had grown so used to the way that the scriptures are seen in my own country that I was surprised and delighted at the response I had over and over again to the Gospels.

How do my own people, twenty-first century Westerners, see the Bible? As something essentially peripheral to life, a quaint pre-scientific leftover that is more or less untrue, but which doesn't really matter anyway. Something that simply doesn't concern me and has no claim on my time or attention.

These people, on the other hand, were interested. They were prepared to give the scriptures the time of day - there was a curiosity and a sense that this was the 'Injil' - something they had heard about but have never seen, and something that they might have been warned against that as good Muslims they should not meddle with, so there is something just a little bit naughty about looking at it. Moreover there seems to be no cringe factor that sense (or fear) that here is this rather threatening person with a Bible open on his lap and any moment now he is going to start preaching at me... No. They were the ones who took the initiative and opened the conversation.

We are helped here by cultural freedoms. On a bus amongst Westerners I am in a private bubble, perhaps doing my own work (as I was trying to do in the taxi). It takes a major event to prick these bubbles and bring people together. Not so in the Middle East or Africa. Public travel is a corporate event; it is a party. Your business is my business. No one would dream of taking out a picnic without offering to share it with the total strangers travelling with you. So the moment it is opened, my Bible becomes public property. Different people in different cultures respond differently, and in Sudan I found that it was much longer before people joined in. Sometimes there was no response, but this was never from inertia; there was simply another agenda - something else was going on, or there was some other topic of conversation to grab people's attention.

I have found this response wherever I have opened my Bible in public in the Islamic world - in coffee shops or government offices in Yemen, the restaurants of Port Sudan, the Kurdish or Somali restaurants of Yorkshire. In Sana'a, the capital of Yemen, there was a tea shop that I visited two or three times a week, and there would always be a gathering of six or seven men there. Scooping up mouthfuls of helba, an iridescent green slime served still boiling in bowls carved from a single stone, they would listen to a story from the life of Jesus while sitting on the table. They would often ask if, by any chance, I had a spare copy of the book that I was reading from that they might take to a friend who might possibly be interested. Usually, as it happened, there was a spare copy or two. One day a policeman wandered over; there was trouble ahead.

The policeman ordered a cup of sweet tea and a bowl of helba, sat down and joined in the discussion.

Once I really did get into trouble. Chatting over a copy of the New Testament with three men in an area that I did not usually go to, I suddenly noticed a tension in the air.

"You'd better leave, those are Ichwaan Muslimeen - the Muslim Brotherhood."

Out of the corner of my eye, standing out in the packed street against a background of men in coloured jackets, knifes strapped to their stomachs, I saw two young men, heads shaved, in white jelabias.

I slipped off and they slipped off after me. I walked faster and so did they. Feeling suddenly very far from home, I broke into a run. The men hitched their jelabias around their waists and ran after me.

I dashed through Sana'a's tiny streets, bumping into veiled women with butane gas bottles on their heads, dodging miniature Fiat flat-tops and camels laden with stale bread. A sudden sense of exhilaration overcame me. It was a John Buchan moment.

I stopped, gasping for breath painfully. The men had given up the chase, or I had managed to lose them. I slowly made my way back to my Land Rover at the Ministry of Health car park, hoping very much that I was not being followed, and reminding myself that I could not expect this activity, entirely legal as it was, to go unchallenged.

Those months in early 1980 were times of heartbreak and joy, mixed together. It had been our heart's desire to join our team in Yemen and after six years at medical school, and training in language and theology, we were at last with the team in that wild, beautiful and medieval country. But by now the team was in trouble, and there were people who were determined to see them evicted from the country. We arrived during a long period of instability, where those who loved the team could keep us in the country, but could not enable us to consolidate and continue the work in child healthcare and midwifery that was our speciality. Those who wanted to see the back of us could stop us working but did not, for many months, have the power to have us finally removed.

It was a time of uncertainty, but a time of great opportunity. I was unable to work as a doctor and complained impatiently, my many years as a student having left me with a longing to just get on with a day's work. I caused endless problems to the team leadership through my immaturity and impatience, and my very slow realisation of what God was doing. I was, however, able to take to the streets - as were a number of others, something that would have been impossible if I had been in demanding medical work. It was a very special time, during which there were endless opportunities and almost miraculous encounters. On two occasions, total strangers came up to me in the street and asked for a New Testament. Waiting for an interview with the Deputy Minister of Health, I casually opened my New Testament in his outer office. Gradually work ceased as his three secretaries left their desks and gathered round. The Minister continued to be delayed, and so the impromptu Bible study continued. Finally I was ushered into his office. Twenty minutes later I left and found the secretaries continuing their reading, in gross neglect of their duties. I muttered my goodbyes and slipped out, leaving them to it.

Others had similar experiences, and a perfect model for this kind of work came from the quiet Australian field leader of the team, whose tasks included the office liaison work that all 'companies' in the Muslim world need to keep them on the right side of the innumerable and ever-changing regulations. Perfectly at ease in Arabic, opportunities to share the Christian Good News seemed to crop up naturally for him all the time in the mundane and tedious bureaucratic situations in which he found himself.

As well as discovering the effect of the Bible on Muslim people, I was discovering something else; how Western our concept of sharing the Good News actually was - and how narrow-minded! I was used to British and American evangelical expressions of the Gospel. At the time, these were essentially step-by-step sequences in which one was asked to accept the claims of Christ, believe in him, trust in his work on the cross, and 'commit your life to him', as I have outlined previously.

As a thoroughly Western-thinking young person this made perfect sense to me. Moreover, I had spent a lot of my childhood at prep school and public school where the Bible was taught routinely. At my public school, 'divinity' was traditionally a high priority, and without noticing it I had painlessly accumulated a rich store of Bible knowledge. Against this background I knew what 'committing my life to Christ' meant, and I did it - as did many of my contemporaries.

However, my whole experience was based on analytical thought-patterns. A method suitable for Western Europe and America, this depends heavily on a residual knowledge of the Bible and of who Jesus is. It also relies on 'assembling' scriptures to fit the step-by-step pattern that I have outlined above, with each step reinforced by proof texts. It is not appropriate for the Muslim world or anywhere else where thought patterns are entirely different and where men and women know nothing of the Christian scriptures or have wrong ideas of who Jesus is.

Here, we were learning something quite different. We seemed to be rediscovering, along with so many others in similar situations, a way of presenting the Good News that came entirely from reading the scripture, allowing the Holy Spirit to do his own work.

We get a clue from Jesus in Mark chapter 14, verses 1 to 19. A woman pours a huge quantity of precious embalming oil over his head. In reply to the mutterings of the bystanders, what does Jesus say?

"I tell you, wherever the Good News is preached, this story will be told in memory of her."

So where is the 'Good News' here? It is the grateful and extravagant response of someone who had come to love and know Jesus, and Jesus' own reaction and acceptance of this profligate woman. In fact it is a narrative, just one of many that go together to make up the picture that we see in the scriptures of who Jesus is. Without this rich library the Good News would make little sense, because we would not know what Jesus was actually like. We would know nothing of his power over wind, waves, disease and demons; his authority to forgive sins; His teaching, both sublime and terrifying; his tenderness to the powerless and the poor; his courage and ferocity in the face of the rich and powerful; his attractiveness; his being sometimes genuinely frightening; his power to command obedience and his power to repel and to make enemies; his deep relationships. We would know nothing of the emotions he called forth, of which this story is an example.

It was Jesus' plan that his work should be understood against the background of his life. "Follow me," he says to Peter, Andrew, John and the others. Much later he says, "but whom do you say that I am?" Peter's response, and the acceptance of the others that Jesus is the Messiah, comes after they have had a chance to be with him, knock around with him, see him at work and at play and in his relationships. Jesus does not leap onto the world stage saying, 'I am the Son of God, believe in me!' No, he lets people get to know him and it is then that the question of who he is begins to come into focus.

A perfect example of this was that of a young English teacher, Abd al Waheed, in Port Sudan. Abd al Waheed and I read the New Testament every night for ten days. Each night he would produce a sentence and demand an explanation. Then we would go on and read. The night before Easter he brought a friend, Nasser. We read the entire Passion account, verse by verse, picking over each phrase and explaining it. We went to bed exhausted after many hours, but they would not let me stop until the very end of John's Gospel.

The next night Abd al Waheed met me alone.

"Jesus is the most wonderful person. Nothing like this has ever happened to me and I must follow him all my life. I know that I must tell my fiancée, and I know that I cannot go on being a Muslim."

We talked all night. I had not mentioned anything about 'becoming a Christian', or 'following Jesus'. Everything had come through the scriptures. The Holy Spirit had introduced and shown Jesus to him, and this almost obsessive, orderly and straightforward young man was overwhelmed - moved to the depth of his being. He had heard the call of Jesus - "Follow me" - just as clearly as the disciples did down by their fishing boats.

Just as deeply affected was Khaldan, another young Sudanese man from a nomadic tribe, the Beja. Khaldan had known people in our mission team during their time in Sudan and had become close friends with team members. When we first met him, his family had become well-off through a soft drinks franchise and by exporting livestock. He invited us to his rich home in Omdurman.

At the evening prayer time, all his friends left the room where we had been chatting and drinking coffee.

"Aren't you going to pray as well?" I asked.

"I never pray," said Khaldan, adding, almost without a pause, "get me a Bible."

The Bible was duly and secretly passed to him as we left. The next day the bell rang at our flat in Khartoum. "I can't read this at home," he said, "it's far too dangerous. Just leave me alone here and let me read."

Khaldan was indeed left alone for several hours. Occasionally my wife crept in with cups of tea. Khaldan was deeply affected by what he was reading. He pressed his fist into his chest as though his heart was in danger of jumping out. "This gives me a great feeling of peace," he kept saying.

Khaldan left his Bible with us and came again the next day. He must have read much of the New Testament in that time, after many hours and many cups of tea. This time we dared to pray. He asked God to help him follow Jesus as he truly wanted to.

I have never known men so deeply affected as these two young Muslims. Each one received a powerful and moving revelation from God entirely through the scriptures, with only a little 'midwifery' from us. We can trust the Holy Spirit to do his own work with the Bible as it is written. We can trust God to reveal his own son, in all his loveliness and holiness, with his own Bible.

Stories and parables

The narrative of Jesus' life reveals him to us as a living breathing character, and as God's son. And in addition, we have his parables and stories. As well as telling us a lot about Jesus himself, his parables and stories add another dimension to our efforts to communicate the Good News.

Parables are interesting. Ask any teacher. When he or she begins a story, eyes light up and people pay attention. When the story is over, they sink back into their chairs - and this is so much more true in story cultures like those across the Muslim world.

Parables engage people. The parable of the Prodigal Son (Luke ch.15 v.11) grips people. There are many prodigals, and this parable can deeply affect the hearts of their parents. I have told this story often and have seen people deeply moved, sometimes to tears.

Parables are political. The parable of the Good Samaritan is both political and social. Jesus graphically points out the deeply racist attitude that the Jews showed towards the Samaritans and, having made the Jewish elite - the priests and Levites - look cowardly and mean, he makes a despised Samaritan the hero of the story.

Parables get the message across. The parable of the unmerciful servant (Matthew ch.18 v.21-35) powerfully underlines the need to forgive others after we ourselves have received totally undeserved forgiveness, and backs up Jesus' command to us to do so. It shows how hard-hearted and ungrateful - and unreasonable - it is to withhold forgiveness from others when we have received so much so freely. It points up this message far more powerfully and memorably than any simple exhortation would have done.

Parables are easily remembered. They stick in the mind of your hearers for many years or a lifetime, and are there for the Holy Spirit to work with.

Parables cross cultural boundaries. Nearly all Jesus' parables are about life at such a basic level that they are universally understandable; marriage feasts, life and death, debt, riches and poverty, greed, farming, sowing and harvest, fishing, boss and employee. They are all accessible to anyone. It is a thrill to see people instantly relating to a story of Jesus, separated as they are by huge time, linguistic and cultural distances. There is no doubt that a knowledge of the culture of the time brings huge depth to our understanding of biblical parables, but the fact remains that their content is so human as to be universally understood.

Parables can be aimed. In the parable of the vineyard (Mark ch.12 v.1-12), Jesus tells the parable of the workers in the vineyard who kill or mistreat the messengers whom the owner sends. Finally the owner sends his son, and the workers kill him too. What will the owner do? He will come and destroy the wicked workers and entrust the vineyard to others. The Pharisees see at once that the story is specifically aimed at them. They are furious enough to plot to kill Jesus.

Parables are incomprehensible. What? We have just spent a lot of time trying to figure out how we can speak to people in a language they can understand, and seeing the confusion that arises when we don't... and you say parables are incomprehensible?

Actually I don't, but Jesus does. Not only that, he says they are deliberately incomprehensible.

His disciples ask Jesus why he speaks to the people in parables (Luke ch.8 v.9). He replies that it is precisely in order that the people should not understand! He quotes Isaiah ch.6 v.9 - "Though seeing they may not see, though hearing they may not understand."

Does this not sound rather harsh and unreasonable? What was Jesus saying?

Part of the answer to this lies in the response of the disciples themselves. They do not understand the parable so they ask Jesus to explain it; and Jesus does. There is absolutely nothing to prevent people from elbowing their way to the front and saying, "I don't understand a word you are saying; I need an explanation." Along the way Jesus does quite a lot of explaining - not only to his disciples but to those who were with him as well. He never refuses to explain when asked. The determined seeker finds; the one who demands an answer will get one. The casual hearer will not.

In addition, the unsolved parable can lodge in the brain for the hearer to work on. It asks a question. Some will work on the unanswered question, and some will ignore it.

Parables are flexible. We read that the parable of the Pharisee and the tax collector was directed at a specific group of people. "To some who were confident of their own righteousness and looked down on everyone else, Jesus told this parable" (Luke ch.18 v.9). It must have had terrific impact, because it is told on their home ground - the practice of worship in the Temple - which all his hearers knew intimately and took part in. The parable was about what they actually did.

It seems arguable that we can use this parable in any context that we choose. We can tell the parable to anyone who is unfamiliar with the practice of worship in the Jewish Temple, and it will have much less impact. But we can tell the same parable with a different venue.

After all, Pharisees have no monopoly when it comes to hypocrisy. Perhaps our hearers are good Church of England people. The worshipper goes to his church saying, "Thank you, Lord, that I am not like other people, who never go to church, look at pornography, fiddle their tax returns...or even like that betting shop owner over there...I come to church every Sunday, my children go to Sunday School, I am even on the church council. I put my envelope into the collection bag without fail every Sunday."

Or perhaps we are having a conversation with Muslims, in which case the worshipper goes to his local mosque.

"Thank you, Allah, that I am not like this man over there who has just come out of prison," he says. "I fast rigorously during Ramadan, I pray five times a day, I would never eat pork or drink alcohol..."

When the story is told on the home ground of the person we are talking to, the impact is far greater: we are pointing up the particular religious observances that are held dear - the places and practices that are relied-on and familiar. When the hearer goes to his church or mosque he may remember the story, which he may not do if he hears the original version.

The irony is that whatever the context of the hypocrite, the 'tax collector' is the same. He is so deeply repentant that he stands at the very back, eyes cast down. He sees himself as he is, pleading for mercy. Here is the classic archetypal posture of the repentant sinner. This picture is universal, whatever culture our hearer comes from.

Do we have the flexibility or the freedom to make changes to the details of the story, as I have done above? Can we 'translate' the parable of the Good Samaritan in the same way, into an equivalent racist context as the original, but in our own time and place? I am sure we can.

Parables encourage discussion. It intrigues me that this, the parable of the Pharisee and the tax collector, is one of the few parables that Jesus follows with an explanation. The answer that the 'repentant sinner' is the one who is acceptable before God may be obvious to us, but people argue over it. Why should the Good Muslim who fasts not be justified before God? What has the tax collector done to deserve God's mercy? Much good work is done when people discuss the parable and argue over its meaning.

There are two stories, or parables, in this book; the story of Ahmed at the very beginning, and the account of the Roundians and the Squarians in Chapter 8. They are intended to suggest that stories have a power to persuade that is sometimes more convincing than arguments can be - however sound they are - and that they are also more entertaining. I include them to emphasise the power of parables and stories. The parables of Jesus are there for us to enjoy and use.

A fierce argument was raging in a meeting in a town in Sudan. The church clinic had been running only a few weeks and was just keeping its head above water. The diocese was already taking money out of the clinic income. I was outraged, but others saw things quite differently. The discussion was lively, loud and acrimonious.

In a moment of silence, and with perfect timing, a voice spoke up. "You can't milk a baby goat on the day it is born." It was immediately obvious to everyone that the clinic needed to grow before being used as a source of income. A parable succeeded where argument had failed.

The Gospel midwife

It seems that God almost invariably requires a midwife to be present at someone's birth as a Christian, and also at other times. Philip is suddenly whisked away from the whirlwind of the Spirit's activity in Caesarea in Acts chapter 8 verse 26 - the Ethiopian eunuch in his chariot is reading the Bible, but he freely admits that he does not understand a word. He is attracted to the scriptures, so he does not discard it in disgust, but starts asking questions immediately. Philip, beginning at the place where the Eunuch is at, explains the Good News of Jesus.

John was sitting on the countertop in his shop in South Sudan, reading his Bible during a slack moment. I asked him, "Do you understand what you are reading?"

"How can I with no one to explain it to me!" said John. I seemed to remember hearing that somewhere else. And Abd al Waheed had said the same thing. In fact he had tried hard to read the New Testament on his own, but on at least one occasion gave up because he could not find anyone to explain it.

It seems that on many occasions God does not use the scripture exclusively, but wishes to involve his people in his work. Once they are involved it seems that God uses the interplay of his written word and the presence of his sons and daughters to press on with his work in the hearts of those who are looking for him. I am sure that there are many Muslim people who have tried to read the Gospel and are waiting for a son or daughter of God to be a midwife to their new life. I enjoy this analogy because the midwife 'attends' the birth and she has a most important role; but she is entirely aware that the work is not hers.

As a junior doctor I attended many births over a six-month period. There was always a deep joy that never seemed to pall. Every birth was entirely different - I had the sense that I was present at an event that was hugely significant, and that I had a very tiny but somehow significant part to play. But the miracle was the mother's. She had done it.

It is a very good metaphor. I had seen a Muslim young man come to faith in Christ in a scruffy delivery room in a tiny hospital in Sharjah, in the United Arab Emirates. I had the same sense that it was not my work at all, but that instead I had been given the extraordinary privilege of witnessing it; and more, that I had been given a tiny but significant part. By my very presence I was reminded forcibly that this was a wonderful work of God in which I should have no part...yet somehow my presence mattered. It gave me a huge thrill.

How does this add up? Mission is not something we as Christians do. It is what God does - and yet he gives us a significant part in it that is not easy to define.

Under the polythene bags and discarded plastic drinks bottles lies the single-track railway that travels through the centre of a town in Sudan. Twice a day the goods train hoots and rumbles its way through town at 12 miles per hour. Across the tracks, the nomads have moved in from the desert and made their home here in Daim al Arab. Climate change and the destruction of their desert economy have forced these people into the town, bringing their camels, cows and goats with them. They speak a language that is quite distinct from Arabic, which puts them at a further disadvantage.

I used to go to Mohammed's cafe in Daim al Arab after a morning's work at the government hospital. Wedged between the camel market, a host of street stalls and the bus stop, Mohammed's was one of a group of eating places where you could get futoor, the meal the Sudanese eat roundabout midday when work finishes. Here you could get commonia, an eye-wateringly fierce-tasting broth made with goat's intestines, and Jabana, coffee with ginger so powerful and sweet that when you left town you had a withdrawal headache. The air reeked of camel dung, coffee and diesel fumes. Men squatted on the ground and on rickety benches, their swords slung over their shoulders and their Jimi Hendrix big hair matted with fat. Culturally it was a huge challenge to me. I had to talk football, about which I know nothing. When Manchester United or Real Madrid were playing, and when there was electricity, the dusty TV was wheeled out from under the table. All life stops for football in Sudan, and Mohammed was mystified that although British, I had heard of almost none of the players he could name.

One such morning I found that I was paying for my own Jabana, a sign that I had achieved some degree of acceptance. I took a very deep breath and started out in Arabic: "I would like to read you something out of God's Book, about Issa the Messiah," I said. And quickly, before anyone had time to object, I started to read the story of the man born blind, from chapter 9 of John's Gospel, and followed it with the good shepherd of chapter 10. There was absolute silence while I was reading and for some moments after. Then someone said quietly, "We must hear more of this," while another murmured, "We need these stories in our own language."

From then on I made it a habit to go down to Daim al Arab with Sudanese pastors and other church people. Coming as they did as displaced people from South Sudan the cultural divide was enormous, but we would sit down and open our Bibles. Most of the men we spoke to coped well in Arabic and the southerners' Arabic was far better than my own. There would be a short Bible reading, and then the reader or someone with him would tell the story informally in his own words. We soon discovered that an open Bible excited curiosity and discussion, sometimes very lively. Arguments would take place, and it was here that I first heard sustained criticism of Islam by Muslims in public. There was always interest, and as people dispersed or moved on to discuss other matters, one or two would occasionally ask, "I have a brother (friend) who would be really interested in this, do you have a spare copy?" The request would come coupled with the invariable refrain that this book was needed in their own language.

We developed this - rather simple - way of doing things further when we were in Egypt. Ibrahim is a pastor in the Episcopal Church in Sudan who is working with some of the many poor Sudanese refugees in Cairo. Ibrahim needed to collect some pictures that he was having framed. At midnight punctually our church meeting ended and we made our way to the shop. After the arrival of tea a lively and rather unproductive confrontation ensued about whether Jesus was the Son of God or not. It seemed that we were stepping into all the pitfalls that I has spent years trying to avoid. Would these three young men read the Injil? "Certainly not," they said cheerfully.

Most providentially the pictures were not ready, and we arranged to go the next night, again at midnight. This time we tried a different tack. Ibrahim agreed to read a story from the Gospel of Luke, from chapter 5 verse 17 -

the story of the paralysed man - and I would follow this up with the story in my own words.

When tea arrived I asked if we could read to them. I produced my ornate and imposing Arabic version of Luke's Gospel, with its red and gold covering in the style of serious Islamic texts. Ibrahim read the story and they listened without interruption. I then told the story freely in my own words. The young men laughed at the idea of the man being lowered through the roof, and listened soberly and thoughtfully to the rest of the story. Where did this story of Issa come from? Why, from the Injil! The men plied us with questions and asked Ibrahim to return; they wanted to hear more of the Injil, the very book they had refused to look at the night before. We left, but the door was opened and the way paved for future visits.

This little episode illustrates perfectly the way that the Christian worker and the child of God is the servant of the Good News. The midwife is there, and is required long before delivery to introduce and read the Bible, and to allow the character and work of Jesus to be revealed in the Gospel narrative. It also illustrates how destructive confrontation can give way to fruitful communication.

Alongside the eagerness with which some people looked at the scriptures was the opposition some people felt. I visited a Somali restaurant in Yorkshire with a Somali New Testament, of which I could read not a single word. The owner was a one-time refugee now established in Britain. He picked up my book.

"What's this?" he said.

"These are the life and words of Issa the Messiah."

"Where did you get this?" he said angrily. "Tell me who translated this and I will kill him tomorrow! Please leave and take it away!"

I explained that things didn't work quite like that in Britain. "Your restaurant is a public place and I have a perfect right to be here and bring in any book I like."

The next day I returned.

"You're not coming in here with that book again," he roared.

I explained that I was coming in and there was nothing he could do to stop me.

After a few noisy confrontations of this kind we became good friends; but he never wanted to look at the Gospel for himself.

Reading the Bible narrative introduces the Good News in its proper context. There is no 'Gospel formula' that exists apart from the living God and his son. Furthermore, as I have explained earlier, Muslims are frequently taught ideas about the Father and the Son that make the Good News incomprehensible - and even untrue - unless we can untangle the confusion. There is no better way to straighten out these false ideas than by letting men and women read the Bible narratives that introduce the Father, Son and Holy Spirit in an interesting and compelling narrative. If, like the Ethiopian eunuch, John and countless others, they admit that they do not understand what they are reading, then the midwife has a role in explaining things.

Yet sometimes - many times - real understanding just does not seem to come. I have, in the last year or two, been involved with several men who have just not 'got it' even after weeks of consistent Bible reading and explanation that have clearly been enjoyed. Mohammed and I met frequently in a cafe. He came with typed lists of questions, underlined and highlighted, that arose out of his Bible reading. We struggled with these on several occasions, and I wondered if he was as exhausted as I was after an hour or so of intense discussion and too much coffee. But nothing seemed to have 'worked' for him. Was the Holy Spirit not at work? I am heartened by Jesus' words: "My father is always at his work, and I too am working."

Rafiq is a middle-aged Sudanese friend. We met weekly to hang out, watch the al-Jazeera news channel for the latest news of Sudan, eat together and read Luke's Gospel. Sometimes there were others present and we didn't get round to our Bible read; sometimes they were there and we read anyway. We thrilled to the miracles and words of Jesus; there were seemingly no pitfalls and no worries about the truth of the Bible. Then came the Passion and death of Jesus - and shutdown.

Was the time wasted? No. Much good work was done, our friendship was strengthened. And the door is open for future encounters with any Christian he might meet.

This demonstrates the many heartbreaks that lie along the way. I am so grateful that it is not my job to transform people. It takes a crucifixion and the work of the Holy Spirit to do that.

Chapter 11

Question Encounters

The New Testament is full of question-encounters between Jesus, his disciples and his enemies. "Who do people say that I am?...but who do you say that I am?" says Jesus to his disciples. "If David called the Messiah 'Lord', how then can he be his son?" says Jesus to the Pharisees.

People do their best to ambush Jesus with questions: "Is it lawful to pay tribute to Caesar?" say the Pharisees who have come to trick him, and later they bring a woman caught in the very act of adultery. They fling her down in front of him: "Moses said such people should be stoned...now, what do you say?"

There are questions that are more sincere. "But who is my neighbour?" "What shall we do to be doing the works of God?"

Some are rhetorical, and not really questions at all: "Lord, to whom shall we go? You have the words of eternal life!" Some are puzzled: "How can a man be born again? How can he enter his mother's womb as a grown man?"

Some are openly confrontational. During an open public teaching session in the temple, a posse of Pharisees and teachers of the law march up to the front. "By what authority do you do these things?" they demand. Jesus' reply is to face them down with another question that puts them in an impossible position: "John's baptism - was it from God or was it human?" They retire in confusion. How the crowd must have enjoyed that.

This feisty interaction contrasts sharply with many of our encounters with Muslims, who often use polemic as we have discussed earlier. It is all too easy, when faced with a long speech, to slip into the same genre, to respond in the same fashion and counter our Muslim friend with argument. When this turns out to be a fruitless battle we may become confused and frustrated.

The temptation to respond to like with like must be resisted. In fact it seems that the polemic style in Islamic culture is really for religion and politics. Less formal conversation contains question and answer as a form of banter. So by moving into a questioning mode we are moving to a more normal, day-to-day way of speaking.

Many times Muslims have asked me a question with the aim of getting a conversation going. We have already discussed the power of questions in Chapter 2, and we need to explore the world of questioning a little more.

As we have seen earlier, this polemic can arise out of your friend's need to justify himself to you, to his friends, and to himself, as a good Muslim who is well able to contend for the faith. This may be his persona - the person he really wants to be seen as by himself and others - but it may not be what he is like at all.

We have also seen that this method of defending and preaching Islam reflects the way that Muslims tend to be taught, and we have also looked at the Islamic philosophy of education, which is entirely alien to Western methods. In turn, this strangeness comes from a pre-Enlightenment way of thinking that accepts the word of authority without question. Muslims are not, on the whole, challenged about, or able themselves to challenge, their Muslim upbringing and education. There is a traditional Hadith that (roughly translated) says, "Don't discuss and don't argue." Even today, many religious teachers come from Pakistan or other Muslim countries where questioning is not part of a child's education. Rote learning - in all subjects, not just Islam - is the preferred and perhaps only teaching method.

They then teach British Muslim kids in the same way as they would in their home countries - by rote.

We need to move into a different kind of encounter, and one way to do this is to ask questions, just as people did in Jesus' time.

However, there are some things which questions are not good for.

Questions are not to score points. We are not there to score anything.

Questions are very definitely not to show up people's ignorance, especially in a group setting where people might be shamed.

Questions are not asked to get answers. Actually this is often the last thing you want. It is often good to ask a question when you part company: "Hey, before you go...I have a question for you think about..." This means that your friend cannot give you an answer then and has the opportunity to think it over privately instead.

Most importantly, we do not ask questions to demonstrate our own knowledge.

So what are questions for?

Questions are to make people think! Dr Faisal was a lecturer at the university where I was enjoying postgraduate studies at the ripe old age of 48. He gave fascinating seminars on the Qur'an. Once I asked him, "It seems to me that you authenticate the Qur'an by citing the Prophet Muhammad, but conversely you authenticate the Prophet by citing the Qur'an...so which comes first, and which is the basis that proves the other?"

"I'll think about it," he said.

In the course of time the episode slipped out of my mind. Imagine my surprise when, over two years later, he came up to me at the graduation tea party. " I am still working on your question but I haven't found the answer yet," he smiled. I was stunned. How could this question have lodged in his mind and bugged him for so long? I realised how a question can get under a person's skin. Questions make people think.

Questions are to get people off religion and onto themselves. How easy it is to get into a discussion about religion - and how pointless! But a well-aimed question will shift the focus of your conversation away from the religion to the person. When you die, will you be going to Heaven or to Hell? This bears directly on a person's relationship with God, a question of existential importance - but most people will indicate to you that they do not know the answer. I have asked this question many times, and the almost invariable response is something like, "We can't know what God actually thinks of us," or "No one, not even the Prophet, can know whether he is going to Heaven or to Hell." This will hopefully spark off a discussion: "But isn't it vital for each one of us to know what is going to happen to us? To know what God thinks of us and how he will deal with us? Here am I, a tiny individual in a vast universe that has existed for billions of years and will exist for billions more - what is to become of me in it?" Your friend may be incredulous that you are sure of where you are going and may, in due course, ask you to explain why. But he may not. Questions do not produce automatic results.

Questions are helpful in stopping a rant. Your friend is in full swing. He is unstoppable and is preaching Islam to you. A question might be the way of causing him to pause. A question or a story may well stop your friend in his tracks.

Questions are a way of challenging or contradicting someone without being confrontational. Your Muslim friend might say, as so many have to me, "You Christians

217

have changed the Bible; it isn't the original Bible at all."
There are many convincing arguments that can be used
to refute this assertion; all doubtless true, and all
equally ineffective. Why? Because there is a vast amount
at stake here; for a Muslim the Bible absolutely must be
untrue. If the Bible is true, Islam is demolished. So your
hearer very much needs to believe this, and you are not
going to convince him.

But there is another reason why argument fails - one
that we have looked at earlier. Our persuasive reasoning
is dashed on the rocks of the pre- Enlightenment,
unquestioning acceptance of authority that is such a
feature of Islamic thinking.

Karim, a sparky 10-year-old, comes to the surgery with
his mother. He picks up the Bible on my desk.

"This has been changed!" he asserts confidently.

"Has it?" I reply, handing it to him, "Show me where!"

"Oh, I don't know, but my teacher at the mosque knows;
you should talk to him."

I am not surprised that Karim cannot back up his
accusation with evidence, but later I visit Karim's
teacher at the mosque. Karim's teacher is also quite

happy to tell me that, "I don't know, but I can tell you someone who does."

The mosque teacher relies on scholarly opinion which he does not challenge. This is medieval or pre-Enlightenment thinking, and it makes our arguments fall on deaf ears.

A more productive way of tackling this very frequent remark might be to ask a question like, "Oh? Tell me more - just how has the Bible been changed and where?"

You may quote a Bible verse and ask whether that particular verse has been altered, or whether it is part of the original. You might also ask how he arrived at this conclusion - in view of the fact that it is a very serious (and actually very offensive) assertion, he must have taken some trouble in assuring himself that it was true. Where is the research, the evidence and scholarship behind this idea? As he may not have the answers to this at his fingertips you might like to remind him in the future of his assertion and that he was going to tell you how he arrived at it!

Many people have said to me, "I don't know the answer, but I know someone who does." My response is, "fine, but you are the one who said it...how about you find the answer from your friend, then you can tell me!"

This will at least show your friend that his opinion is second-hand, and that it is untested. It is more likely to make him think than any scholarly argument. Of course all this is tailored to your own personality, how well you know your friend and how well you get on together.

Listening

Asking questions requires something of extreme importance: we need to listen to the answer, not just so that we can frame a reply, but so that we can hear the person. Listening means that we are honouring the person we're talking to. I have asked the question, so I must listen to the reply. The reply may not reflect what the speaker believes, but he needs to be listened to. Your speaker may give you an answer that saves face and saves the honour of Islam, but he or she will know the truth even if they are not admitting it. We may not believe the answer, but we need to listen. Muslims are crowding into business, medicine, the law and politics. Many are academics. I have met many very bright and intelligent Muslim men and women. What they have to say is worth listening to, even if you are going to argue with them. But even if they do not seem to be particularly bright or educated their answer needs to be treated with respect and consideration, not condescension.

Questions strengthen friendship. As well as being an antidote to rhetoric, your questions will strengthen your friendships, because tactful questioning and answering fosters intimacy and understanding between people, where polemic tears people apart. Hopefully you will wrestle with difficult things together rather than wrestling against each other. I have had many discussions where question and answer have brought mutual enjoyment to the encounter rather than conflict.

Answers are unpredictable. Asking questions is not a technique in itself, and there are no trump cards, no kill-all questions that end the discussion. A lawyer once said, "Never ask a question that you do not know the answer to," and while you may well know the answer to your question, it may not be the answer you get!

Many years ago when I was very new to the Arab world and its ways, I gave a lift to a young man on a desert road in Jordan. We struck up a conversation and we were getting on really well. I turned to him and asked a question I have already mentioned above. "When you die," I said, "where will you go? Will you go to Heaven or to Hell?"

"When I die I shall go straight to Heaven!" he exclaimed. "I am a good Muslim, I do not drink or smoke, I pray regularly, I have been on the Hajj, I give alms. Yes! I shall be in Heaven, praise God!"

This was not at all what I expected to hear. I was speechless. Later I might have told him the parable of the Pharisee and the tax collector, but on this occasion I was nonplussed. This was not at all typical of the answers that I have heard on many other occasions. I learned that one must be on the lookout for any kind of answer - that people are unpredictable, and that asking questions may mean losing control of where you are going.

Questions are dangerous and subversive. Questions should come with a health warning - in fact they should be dangerous; that is their job. We cannot and must not overtly attack Islam or the beliefs of Muslims. This would be rude, aggressive and ineffective. It would destroy our relationships with our Muslim friends and we would lose forever the possibility of sharing the Good News with them. However, our questions are going to be a challenge from the rear on our friends' most cherished beliefs. Well-aimed questions will enable your friend to ask her own questions, unprompted by you, in the secret places of her heart. There are many Muslim men and women in the West who are deeply concerned about their own faith - its nature, particularly its violent character, and its veracity. Your questions will discomfort them still further.

I had occasional discussions with a Muslim colleague at work. There was no doubt that this person was deeply disturbed by Islam and by his place within it. I asked questions when we chatted, but the most aggressive questions asked of him were his own. Questions are insidious, subversive and dangerous. Questions are able to speak to the real person behind the persona. They worm their way into people like straight statements do not. They challenge people, and they challenge the basis of Islam on the only battlefield that really matters, the battlefield of people's hearts.

Questions do not affect everyone. Sometimes we can see a hunger in a person - sometimes it is clear that the Holy Spirit is at work, and they respond positively to questions. Sometimes it is the opposite, and people seem unmoved, and will not engage. This is an act of their own free will, but we cannot and must not write people off. I will never forget the academic who could not let go of the question I had asked him. God is at work in the hearts of countless people, and we know not a thing about it.

We must at all times treat our Muslim friends with kindness and courtesy, and we must not play games. We must not rush in with the Good News the moment our friend is struggling with a question to which he cannot find an answer. Nevertheless, there is a right time to introduce Christ, because he has the words of eternal life. "Why don't we read the Bible together and see if it has any clues?" you might say.

Questions are cultural. Having enjoyed hundreds of conversations with men and women in Muslim cultures, I am convinced that question and counter-question are every bit as normal as polemic, and much more fun. Questions are part of normal friendly chat. I have been asked hundreds of questions by Muslim men and women, and I've learned that in this culture people usually don't want an answer - they want a conversation!

Note; There is a list of questions at the end of this book (Appendix 1) they are intended to indicate the many aspects of Islam and life that we might ask questions about. They are certainly not meant to be used indiscriminately. I have usually ended up just using one or two, though I have used all of them at one time or another.

Chapter 12

The Head Banger

We have looked at this in the previous chapter, and I suggested that asking questions might be helpful; but I have alluded to this problem several times, and we need to look at it in a little more detail.

Many times in my earlier years working in Muslim countries I had unpleasant encounters with ardent Muslims. These conversations were almost invariably with men, and with at least with one or two onlookers. They were almost never tête-à-tête. They were almost always with people I knew little or not at all. The Muslim speaker would be doing about 95% of the talking, and if by any chance I got a word in edgeways, I would be interrupted.

Furthermore, the 'preaching material' would be surprisingly uniform. It is likely, too, that he would have been holding forth as much about the errors of Christianity as the truth of Islam. We were firmly in the 'head' area. Time after time I have been subjected to the same sermon, delivered in an aggressive and assertive tone, and I would go away deeply distressed that I had 'let God down' and that this person had gone away notching up yet another Christian demolished, and more affirmed than ever in his own faith. Many Christian workers have had similar experiences, frequently with the same emotional outcome. 'Why could I not hold my end up?'

What is happening here is a personality struggle that has nothing to do with the Good News and may not have very much to do with Islam either, even though doubtless the talker is deeply convinced of what he is saying. It can be a damaging and unwholesome experience.

So how do we avoid or turn around these encounters?

Let your friend talk

Let the talker talk. There is no harm in his going on for quite a long time. Whatever he says about the Gospel, Christians or the Bible, do not be tempted to argue or contradict, even if he is telling you what Christianity is and why it is so obviously wrong and untrue. This will only add fuel to the flames. Don't even look as though you want to say anything. Sit back and be patient. Relax!

Ask a question

There will eventually come a time when he needs some kind of reaction or response from you. This is your opportunity to ask a question. A good opener is something like this: "I really want you to tell me about Islam, but it would be much easier if you would answer some questions that I have. I feel sure you will have the answers I am looking for."

Your friend is not likely to refuse this opportunity. You then have the chance to get the subject away from Islam, and onto your friend himself. What does God think of you personally? Where will you be going when you die?

You might, on the other hand, want to challenge him to think about his own faith in a new way that is not along the lines which he has been taught. If he has been holding forth about the Bible, and telling you how many errors and inconsistencies one can find there, you might ask a question that cannot be answered without study and thought. "Can you tell me about the character of God as you see it disclosed in the Bible? How does it differ from the way God is portrayed in the Qur'an?

Get one-to-one

We have already talked about the need a person might have to show his friends, himself and you that he is a good Muslim who is well able to uphold his religion and fight for it. Having an encounter with someone on their own frequently results in a different dynamic. The 'Nicodemus' factor comes in here. A Swiss friend recounted to me with huge amusement how two men behaved in the town where he lived in Chad. They were in the habit of denouncing him loudly in the street as a 'Christian missionary,' even ostentatiously avoiding him by crossing over to the other side of the road when they met in the street. Yet these were the very men who were visiting him secretly at night.

If a person is playing to the crowd he may be entirely different when he sees you alone. Sometimes a person will be throwing up a smokescreen when they out on an aggressive act of a good Muslim. Sometimes there is such fear from community and friends that people feel compelled to adopt this kind of behaviour. This 'smokescreening' is not confined to those who are interested in the Gospel. I once asked Robina, a young woman in her twenties why she wore niqab, the full veil, over her face. "I wear it for a quiet life," she said. "Behind it I can think what I like."

Tell a story

Questions are effective in stemming a verbal onslaught, and stories are even more so. In Jordan, which is very much a storytelling culture, I was constantly amazed that a man in full flood could be stopped at once if I offered to tell a story. If there was a break in the flow, whatever the context, I would say "There is a story I would really like to tell you," and I never ceased to marvel at the way people would listen in complete silence. When it was over we would then start talking about the story. Some of the stories of Jesus, like that of the Prodigal Son, are deeply moving, and often there is a prodigal not far away. The conversation shifts from heavy theology to personal experience. The stories of Jesus are arresting and sometimes funny as well - I was reading the parable of the Pharisee and the publican with a young man, and he found the caricatures and exaggeration hilarious. And they are!

Use email

You can't interrupt the written word. Besides, if you can't think well on your feet, this is a ideal way of interacting with a friend who has difficulty listening. Much discernment is needed because you will soon discover that Muslims don't argue in the same way as Westerners, for the reasons I have outlined earlier. Email conversations can go on for months and can be very stimulating, and by their nature tend to be private.

Be ready to withdraw

Sometimes you get nowhere. I once had a bruising encounter with a middle-aged man. He listened in stony silence to the story of the Prodigal Son; at the end he said, "That is not a story from the Bible. You are not telling the truth!" There was little more to say.

In all these encounters there is no magic formula, and in many cases it is better to extricate oneself politely and leave. I was accosted in an airport in Sudan by a school teacher who I had never previously met. I noticed that he had the patch of hard skin in the centre of his forehead which comes from repeated praying and pressing the forehead on the ground. This man insisted on preaching to me at length. Telling me that he was a scholar, and that he knew the Bible far better than I did, he would countenance no questions, nor listen to any stories or words of Jesus. Even when we agreed that we would each have five minutes to speak in turn he could not stick to it. "I am so sorry, but I must interrupt you because you are in error," he said, and in the end I had to politely ask him to leave me alone. In these cases a gracious manner may be your only contribution to what your friend understands about Christians.

In all these encounters my overriding aim is to get away from 'religion' and into things that are personal. Many people love nothing better than to talk of religion. They know their faith well; they are on home ground, and they are confident. In such conversations, we are firmly in the 'head' area. There is nothing so barren and fruitless as talk of religion. We must move the conversation on to the personal. Forget religion - what does God think about you? Where do you stand in front of the living God? These are the questions that are important.

We need to remember that with these bruising encounters we are in the 'head' area, where Islam is strong. Our aim must be to reach the 'gut' level, where conflict is much less likely and where there is no persona. This takes time, and this is where your relationship comes in. It seems to me that these encounters are more frequent among strangers and rare among friends. When there is a relationship we are beginning to migrate to the 'gut' level.

Chapter 13

The Qur'an

We have discussed the Bible at length, but what about using the Qur'an? I have been a great enthusiast for interfaith dialogue ever since I read the story of Elijah and his contest with the prophets of Baal (1 Kings ch.18 v.16-46). Elijah was content to be outnumbered 450 to 1 - and not only that, but he gave his opponents the entire day to state their case. Elijah never hindered them; in fact he encouraged them. He waited until they had completely run out of steam.

What we have here is of course not a dialogue but a power-encounter. The prophets of Baal needed the whole day on Mount Carmel to show them that their god was simply not there. Muslims need an encounter with the Qur'an for exactly the same reason.

Word made book

We need to remind ourselves that the Bible and the Qur'an are in no sense equivalent. For Christians, Jesus is the 'Word made flesh' to which the Bible points (John ch.1 v.14). For Muslims, as someone has pointed out, the Qur'an is 'word made book'; it is God's final revelation. But the trouble for us is the way Muslims look at the Qur'an, which we have discussed above in Chapter 3.

The 'magical' way of looking at Qur'an means that it is a kind of talisman; it does not actually need to be read and understood for its meaning. Many Muslims do not understand Arabic, and so cannot read the text. Even many Arabic speakers seem to be very unfamiliar with all but a few passages. Some can read and recite it but have spent little time considering its meaning. The emphasis is on learning by heart and recitation, not on understanding, and certainly not on detailed analysis and application. Muslims don't do 'Qur'an study' in the same way that Christians do Bible study. They don't sit around over coffee and biscuits and struggle over the text in the same way.

We have mentioned pre-Enlightenment thinking at the outset. A feature of this kind of outlook is a readiness to accept the opinions and judgement handed down by their elders, imams and scholars without questioning in a way that has not been practiced in Europe and the West for many centuries. This can apply even to second-generation Muslims educated in the West. A blog from an intelligent young Asian lady assures me that Islamic authorities have handed down that Islam is peaceful. She does not feel the need to ask for any evidence or back up to this statement, which would not be acceptable on its own to anyone educated in the West. She goes further and explains that the Qur'an is so deep and complex that its analysis cannot be entrusted to anyone other than eminent and experienced academics and imams. This outlook is anathema to Westerners, who consider that they have a right to call any authority to account. It explains so much of how many Muslims tend to look at the Qur'an. We need to gently help and encourage our Muslim friends to analyse the Qur'an, and render it accountable.

This bar to questioning and analysis by Muslims themselves is the Qur'an's very best defence. As long as it is not read and scrutinised for its meaning, its lack of power and content will be concealed. We must do everything we can to encourage Muslims to read the Qur'an. There are many Christians from Muslim backgrounds who can testify to the Qur'an being their starting point on the journey towards Jesus. Aisha, a young Muslim lady in Birmingham, wanted to read the Qur'an and asked a Christian churchwarden to get her one. Wisely, he agreed. Aisha tells how the lack of content in the Qur'an drove her to look elsewhere for what she craved, and how she then found Christ through the Bible. Shazia, a strong-minded Iranian practice manager in a surgery where I was working temporarily, was reading the Qur'an at night. Before work started she would come and tell me what she had been reading. Most mornings she was incandescent: "I just will not believe this stuff," she shouted one day, after reading about the Prophet's wives. Another day it would be something else. I was watching the Holy Spirit doing a demolition job. Mahmood, a brilliant and charismatic young student in Jordan, searched the Qur'an for something to give meaning to his life. "When I read the Qur'an I realised it had nothing to say to me," he exclaimed. Later we met him in London and he had become a Christian -and being the kind of person who could not possibly keep his faith a secret, found himself in a great deal of trouble on his return to the Middle East. When the Holy Spirit is at work he will do a Mount Carmel on the Qur'an *as people read it*. It is not flammable. Like the altar on Mount Carmel under the pleadings and blandishments of the prophets of Baal, it simply will not catch fire.

The Qur'an's witness to the Messiah

The Qur'an, however, does have a number of references to Jesus, who in it is called 'Issa'. And on at least 10 occasions he is called the 'Messiah'. This is a great mercy, as it prevents Muhammad the Prophet from being given that title. It is also a good subject for a question: "If the Qur'an uses the expression 'Messiah', what does it mean? Why is Muhammad not the Messiah?"

The Qur'an has many things to say about Jesus that give him a unique status in the book. He creates, he will be coming again to judge the world, he was born of a virgin. He is called both 'a word from God' and 'a spirit from God'. These features are not just unique, they are miraculous. The distinctive feature of the life of Issa is the direct intervention of God himself. The miraculous authenticates Jesus and overrides all dissent and argument.

Issa was born of a virgin by a direct creative act of God. S3.47

Issa has the ability to create living beings out of clay. S3.49 Who alone is able to create?

Issa is given God's permission to heal lepers, give sight to the blind and raise the dead to life. S3.49

Issa is spoken of as 'A word from God'. S4.171

Issa is spoken of as 'A spirit from God'. S4.171

At the end of his life on Earth 'God took him to himself', alive. S4.158

Muslims believe that Issa is therefore still living and will come to earth again.[19]

These are true statements (with reservations about the specific meaning of the statement that Jesus was a spirit from God). They are not what preachers call 'saving truth', but they are true as far as they go, and they point to the person who is undoubtedly the greatest person spoken of in the Qur'an. Muslims have no obligation to read the Bible but they are obliged to take their own scripture seriously. They may, of course, ignore the challenge - but nevertheless the Qur'an, like the altar to the unknown god encountered by Paul in Acts chapter 17 verse 23, is a good place to start.

Read it yourself!

If you are to encourage Muslims to read the Qur'an you must have read the Qur'an first. This is likely to be quite

---

[19] The Hadiths; Bukhari Volume 3, Book 34, Number 425; Volume 3, Book 43, Number 656; Volume 4, Book 55, Number 658.

a struggle; the chapters are arranged in order of length, which itself says something about how it was viewed by those who first put it together. There is little of what might be accepted as great literature: there is no character development and no sustained narrative. All hangs on the sound of the Qur'an as it is read, and that is actually what the word Qur'an means: 'The Reading'. Listen to the Qur'an being read in the mosque and you will get the idea, and perhaps you will pick up some of the fervour of its hearers as they listen. Arabic is a language of amazing sounds.

When I am out shopping, I hear the sound of what sounds like a political diatribe coming from the megaphone on an approaching lorry, the words totally obscured by the appalling electronics. The speaker piles cadence on cadence and phrase upon phrase in his passion. When the lorry draws alongside I see that it is the rag-and-bone man calling us to bring out our unwanted domestic bits and pieces. Arabic is a bit like that. The Qur'an, its language and its sound, has an emotional impact entirely separate from the meaning of the words; but it is the words that we need to encourage people to read.

Even if you manage to read the Qur'an, your problems are not over. Most translations into English are rounded and softened to moderate the fierceness of the original. The translation most used in Britain is that by Yusif Ali. He translates the word 'rab' as 'cherisher', but the word actually means 'Lord'. Obviously a key word, this meaning is found in no dictionary and gives a totally false slant to the meaning. The Yusif Ali version is commonly read by Muslims who cannot read Arabic and who consequently get a false impression of what the Qur'an actually says. Some versions are written in seventeenth-century English even though they appeared in the twentieth century. Some are simply incomprehensible.

A place to start

Nevertheless, we must start where our Muslim friends are, just like Paul did in Athens. But like Paul we do not stop there. We can suggest to our Muslim friend that as a good Muslim and someone who takes the Qur'an seriously, he might like to consider what the book says about Jesus. How many prophets are there? Many. How many Messiahs? One! Of the many prophets how many were miraculously born of a virgin? One! Is this of no significance? Why was the life of Jesus so miraculous, and unlike any other? All these are questions can point to the New Testament. As a good Muslim, would you like to learn more about the Messiah that the Qur'an talks about so much? How about you and me reading the New Testament together? We can explore the extraordinary life of Issa in detail together and see what 'Messiah' really means.

With Shazia and Mahmoud we can see the impact of reading the Qur'an on those who have broken free of the constraints of pre-Enlightenment thought patterns. We need to pray and work to enable future generations of Muslims, educated in the West, to be free to access the Qur'an, to see what it says about Jesus, and to move on from there to the Gospels.

Chapter 14

Using Words

As St Francis said, we need to use words. Jesus himself is the Gospel; he is the Good News and he is the way, the truth and the life - but he tells us to get out there and communicate this. And to do that, we need to speak the Good News in a language that our hearers can understand, have in mind some of the wrong ideas that are in the minds of our hearers. In this chapter, my aim is rather to look at the Good News from the perspective of the many misconceptions and prejudices that your Muslim friend will have in his or her mind - in particular the deficiencies inherent in the Islamic view of God - and to suggest ways to work through them.

I have used headings because that is how my Western mind works. Categories like this can be useful, but the last thing we need to do is to use categories with our hearers, who, as we have seen, may have an entirely different mental framework (and besides this, some of them are Christian technical terms). Nor need we communicate these truths in a set order, or all at once. Jesus never had a set way of talking to people - everyone was treated as an individual. It is enough if, as we engage in our daily relationships, we bear in mind that at some stage we need to articulate these things, preferably when asked and during normal conversation. When we read the Bible together there will be lots of opportunities to cover what we call 'The Gospel' - the verbal way we communicate who God is, what his attitude is to us, what he has done for us, how we can respond, and what the consequences of our response will be. Simply put, we will have plenty of chances to share God's rescue plan.

God

"But God isn't like that - God doesn't love, he is above that kind of thing!" A group of medical students were arguing with me after a workshop. "But I have some fantastic news for you," I replied. "That's just what God is like!"

This is where the rescue plan starts. We have seen that the concept of God in Islam makes nonsense of the idea of any rescue plan. These young men and women can never hope to understand the plan if they have a wrong view of God, and without love there can be no Good News. But God has a deep and passionate commitment to men and women. What mother, seeing her little daughter fall into a river, will not instantly fling herself in after her to save her life? And the Bible tells us that even if the impossible happens and a mother forgets her child, God cannot forget his (Isaiah ch.49 v.15). This is backed up not only by words but by his actions in taking the initiative and rescuing his people. The very use of the word 'mother' to explain the depth of God's love for us tells us that relationships are at the very heart of God. So often, our Muslim friends can find God's rescue plan incomprehensible because the God of Islam is non-relational, non-loving and not at all sacrificial. Having said this, I sometimes encounter men and women who have a deep sense that God is approachable, that he cares for them, and that he answers prayer when they cry out to him. This is not true Islam; but it is what God is like.

"God will love you if you love him," said Ali to me after a long discussion. But if God is truly God, surely his behaviour is not dependent on what I do? The God we see in Jesus always acts according to his own character, not according to mine. It is he who takes the initiative, not me. That is part of the Good News.

But God is also holy, terrifyingly good, and absolutely pure; hating evil with a deep and terrible hatred. Try reading the book of Deuteronomy with your friend (yes, not easy but you would be surprised!) - this book plays out the tension between the God's love and his wholehearted commitment to his people on one hand, and on the other his hatred of any kind of wrong.

It is this problem that God's rescue plan exists to solve.

Sin

God hates all wrongdoing, but how do we communicate the seriousness of this? My Muslim friends do not see 'sin' as a serious problem. "God is merciful and forgiving," they tell me. And a rescue service is no use to anyone who does not need a rescue. "Great news, the fire engine is on its way!" is not great news if you do not know that your house is on fire. In fact, it is more likely to cause anxiety and confusion than relief. To tell someone that there is a great rescue plan for them, and that they can have the bad things in their own heart dealt with, is no great news unless it is recognised for what it is; an offer to save them from something that is serious, that is life threatening.

Fortunately we don't have to solve this particular communication problem. Jesus has done it for us.

One day Peter asks Jesus how many times he is obliged to forgive his brother when he wrongs him. Jesus tells him a story about debt (Matthew ch.18 v.21), which he uses elsewhere. It is very closely connected with sin, and is more than just imagery (Matthew ch.6 v.12). Few of your friends will have lain awake at night worrying about the bad things in their life, but nearly all of us have problems and worries about money. Muslim or not, we are at once immersed in real life experience.

The story Jesus tells Peter in Matthew 18 starts with a king who calls his servant to account. The king has absolute authority over the servant, who owes the king an impossibly huge sum of money. His inability to pay means that the consequences are catastrophic. His life and his family will be destroyed.

Jesus show us in the clearest possible terms where we stand in front of an all-powerful God to whom we must give account, shows us that our indebtedness is infinitely beyond anything we can repay, and describes the consequent judgement. Our situation, like that of the servant, is dire. The problem of sin is really the problem of what God is actually like.

But that is not where it ends. When the servant pleads for mercy he gets not a reprieve but complete release, with no strings attached whatsoever. The king, as well as being all-powerful, is compassionate and generous. He cancels the debt and the servant goes free.

What does your Muslim friend think is going on here? The question that begs to be asked is this: "who pays?" After a moment's thought it is clear: the king pays every penny. The king is worse off to the value of the massive sum that he has written off. The king forgives the debt at huge cost to himself. With debt this is far easier to see than with sin, where it might not be at all clear that it has to be paid for. Jesus is telling us that this is what God is like. The character of God is both the cause of the problem and its solution. His authority and holiness require that the debt is paid. His mercy and compassion demand that the king himself pays.

There is more. The servant walks into the king's presence under a law that everyone in any culture understands. Money borrowed has to be paid back. But he leaves under another completely different law, which does need explanation. The debt is freely forgiven so the servant is obliged to live from now on under this new law, the law of forgiveness - the law of getting what you do not deserve. This is what Christians call 'grace'.

This is immediately obvious to us and to the other servants in the second part of the story, who are outraged at the first servant's behavior when another servant owes him money. Should he not have run up to his fellow worker immediately shouting "Good news! The king has forgiven my entire debt - and I am forgiving what you owe me!" But no, he acts without mercy, even though the debt owed to him is tiny compared with what he owed to the king.

The story Jesus tells ends with the desperate fate of the first servant, who is both ungrateful and unreasonable. The failure to forgive when one is already forgiven negates the original forgiveness of the king and flies in the face of his kindness and sacrifice. The servant ends where he began, helpless in the face of the king's judgement. We also end the story where we began, with the words of Lord's Prayer: "Forgive us our debts as we forgive our debtors."

This short story highlights nearly all we need to know about sin - the awesome God to whom we must give account, the irretrievable depth of our predicament, our own helplessness, the huge mercy and kindness of God, who forgives at great cost to himself; the triumph of grace over the law of 'pay back what you owe,' and the absolute requirement that the one who is forgiven forgives in turn, with failure to do so negating all the forgiveness so freely received.

If you read this with your Muslim friend they might begin to see the problem of sin through Jesus eyes. There is one missing link in Jesus' parable, however, as we will see later on.

Substitution

"No one can pay for what I have done wrong except me! That's unfair..."

So many Muslim friends find the idea of substitution a stumbling block. The Qur'an itself suggests that someone was substituted for Jesus on the cross at the last minute, which turns the whole idea of Christ's death for us on its head. One might ask one's Muslim friend what they think is going on here. Why did God make it look as though Jesus was on the cross when it was in fact someone else? And where is the justice in that?

In fact the idea of substitution is well established in our sense of fairness and justice, and we can illustrate this to our friends easily. There is one particular story that I enjoy and use often. I believe it is true, though I have never discovered its origin. In fact it does not need to be historically true; as a drama it only needs to impress upon the hearer the only possible resolution to the problem it poses.

A Mexican bandit chief and his gang of thugs were accustomed to raiding villages then carrying off possessions and livestock. There came a time when the villagers got wise to what was going on. Time and again they managed to beat off the raiders.

The bandit chief realised that someone was warning the villagers of the impending raids; that someone had to be within the group and aware of where the next raid would be. The chief called his men together and angrily announced that someone was warning the villagers. He declared that when the culprit was found he would be flogged mercilessly.

Imagine the consternation of the chief when his mother confessed that it was none other than herself.

The chief is faced with a dilemma. If he lets his mother off, what will the bandits think? They will be quick enough to say that if it had been one of them they would have been flogged to within an inch of their life. To withhold the flogging would be a manifest injustice. On the other hand he cannot possibly stand there and see his mother whipped.

The chief solves the problem by receiving the punishment in his own body. He steps up there in the place of his mother who goes free.

This story powerfully illustrates the dilemma. The demands of family and love, and the demands of justice, are incompatible. Neither can be set aside. They can be reconciled only through substitution. Anyone who hears this story is forced to that conclusion. I have never heard anyone disagree that the chief's course of action is self-evidently right and satisfies both the demands of justice from the robbers and the demands of family from himself.

Moreover, this story points up the nobility of the chief, criminal gang leader though he is. To substitute oneself into the place of one who in no way deserves it is a heroic act.

There is a further story, about a sheikh, the head of a family, which comes from the legends of a people group in eastern Sudan. It is all the more powerful as it speaks out of the tradition of giving hospitality and refuge that is deeply woven into that culture, and of the equally strong tradition of family honour, both of which are so characteristic of Muslim peoples. I quote the original in full.

"A man fleeing from a murder he had committed took refuge in the house of Abdul Latif. The relatives of the dead man, intent on their revenge, followed the killer to his sanctuary and demanded that he be surrendered.

Abdul Latif tried every means to save the refugee, offering generous compensation, but the relatives of the dead man were unmoved and insisted that unless Abdul Latif gave them the murderer, they would drag him by force from Abdul Latif's dwelling and slaughter him on the threshold.

At this Abdul Latif consented to speak with them privately, and taking them to a distance he said, "What you propose to do would forever disgrace me and pollute my house, but since you insist on this man's blood, I will show you the tree under which he spends the night and thus you can come on him unawares as he sleeps, and take him."

The relatives of the dead man somewhat reluctantly agreed to this plan, and having made sure of the exact spot they departed.

All that day Abdul Latif spent dividing up his wealth in money and animals and in giving his children his last words of advice, for he had decided to lay himself down beneath the fatal tree. In doing this, he would pay for the crime of the murderer who had taken sanctuary in his house. But his son, discovering his purpose, refused to allow his father to carry it out, insisting that he would take his father's place beneath the tree and so uphold their family honour.

That night as the relatives of the dead man were on their way to the appointed spot, one of their number was visited by doubts that Abdul Latif, that soul of honour, would so sacrifice anyone who had taken refuge in his house. He told his companions of his doubts, and urged them to make sure that whoever they found under the tree was the man they sought before they killed him.

And so the son of Abdul Latif was discovered, and the murdered man's relatives were so impressed with the magnanimity of Abdul Latif that they gave up their plan of vengeance and spared the life of the murderer.

Again, the demands of honour and revenge are satisfied by substitution. This is another illustration of 'grace'.

These two stories illustrate the heroism of the one who offers himself as substitute for someone utterly undeserving. There are many others. We can now move on to see that the action of Jesus on the cross was the action of a hero of the highest order, and self-evidently just. He offers himself in substitution because it is the only way that the demands of the judgement of God and

252

his love can be reconciled. It is the only answer to the problem of evil that does not result in the deserved condemnation of the sinner.

Grace

"But it's too easy!" Basim, a young university lecturer was firing questions at me as we hurtled along the motorway on our way home.

Deep down in nearly all of us is the conviction that we don't get anything unless we work for it. Coupled with this, we need to be masters of our own fate. "I may live or die, but there is not a thing I can do about it either way," is a hard pill to swallow.

So I have to explain gently to Basim that it is not easy, and it is not difficult. It is impossible. I might conceivably swim 20 miles if I train hard. But if I fall off the Titanic I cannot swim the remaining 2000 miles of freezing water to New York. I can possibly jump out of a burning house, but in the inferno at the top of the World Trade Centre I am going to die if I am not rescued. My fate is out of my hands. It is a matter of perspective. This is where we look at the parable of the king and his steward. Possible things are easy or difficult. Impossible things are impossible. That is why the Good News is not a work-hard-for-it service. It is a rescue service, and Jesus is called a rescuer.

God's answer to our impossible predicament is grace. This is easy to explain and hard to accept. The bandit chief and the Sudanese sheikh with his code of honour are in the same predicament brought about entirely by their own character. The bandit could easily have told his men that his mother was just not going to get punished and they had better get their heads round it. Abdul Latif could have taken the easy way out and allowed the fugitive to be dragged out and killed on his doorstep. What was to prevent these two outcomes? Their honourable character.

In exactly the same way the character of God demands that he behave in the same way to us. God loves his creatures. More, he identifies with them to an extent that is hard to imagine. He also is a God of justice and holiness who cannot look at wickedness and wrong.

Jesus, in his stories, gives as an insight into the character of God that starts to make sense of grace. He tells us about an employer who continually hires men throughout the day (Matthew ch.20 v.1-16). The men hired first thing in the morning are paid a day's wage, but the men hired later at intervals are offered the same wage, with the last on board doing barely an hour's work. When it is pay-time the first to be hired are outraged, and one can easily see why - whatever they were offered, the outcome is not fair. But that is precisely the point; grace is not fair! The men hired at the end of the day get a day's wage for hardly any work. This parable illustrates beautifully the unreasonableness of Gods character, for grace is essentially unreasonable. It also illustrates how easy it is for us to resent the grace that is given to others. The father of the dissolute and wayward son shows the same characteristic (Luke ch.15 v.11-32). The young man comes home, utterly undeserving of anything. His father's reaction is entirely out of proportion. What is reserved for a once-in-a-decade festival is at once 'squandered' on this undeserving wretch. The only explanation is the character of the father who chooses to regard this individual as a son who has figuratively come back from the dead rather than as someone who has wasted half of his family's fortune.

"It's too easy!" is the feeling that sits behind the objection of the hard working men in the vineyard, and the faithful older brother who is furious at his young brother's reception. "We have earned it! We are outraged that others have got what we've got and don't deserve it!"

Quite so. But that is not how God operates. That is not his character. No one is entitled to anything from God. He owes nobody anything. Everything is from his boundless generosity, by grace. Jesus illustrates his father's boundless liberality in his own life. His healings without number, the vast over-production of bread at the feeding of the crowds (John ch.6 v.1-15), the shocking over-supply of superb quality wine for men and women who had already had enough to drink (John ch.2 v.1-11), and finally the giving of his own life.

Once in a very daring moment Moses said to God, "show me your glory." (Exodus ch.33 v.18). God's reply was to show Moses not a firework display or a spectacle, but the very heart of his character. God passes by Moses, declaring "The Lord, the Lord; the compassionate and gracious God, slow to anger, abounding in love and faithfulness, maintaining love to thousands and forgiving wickedness rebellion and sin. Yet he does not leave the guilty unpunished." (Exodus ch.34 v.6).

What? There is an absolute contradiction in these sentences. They cannot both be true. How can God forgive wickedness, rebellion and sin without leaving the guilty unpunished?

The answer of course is the answer of the bandit chief and the Sudanese sheikh. The demands of love and judgement can only be met by God himself receiving the punishment rightly deserved by the guilty. Here is the grace of God demonstrated to the full. God, in revealing his glory and his character, at the same time reveals the problem of evil. This contradiction is only resolved hundreds of years later, and many pages further on in your Bible, in the death of Christ.

The cross

So how is the cost actually paid? As we saw above, the story of the ungrateful servant has one missing ingredient. The principle in the story is 'money for money'. But the penalty for wrongdoing is death. How can it be otherwise? The principle now becomes 'a life for a life'. "The son of man came...to give his life as a ransom for many," says Jesus (Matthew ch.20 v.28). Debt is paid for with money, but sin is paid for with blood. Money for money, and life for life.

There is no avoiding the cross; it is the central fact and feature of God's rescue plan and the stumbling block that many Muslim people fall over. It sometimes seems that there are unseen forces that rise up within our Muslim hearers to cause huge resistance at this very point. But whatever language we use, whatever love we show, whatever our relationship is like, however many glorious answers to prayer we see, we need to confront the cross: the death of Christ, his payment for 'wickedness, rebellion and sin'. That is what the Good News is about. Moreover, if there is no death there can be no resurrection, which is the central miraculous act of God which divinely authenticates God's rescue plan.

Sometimes when the Holy Spirit is at work there is simply no problem. Khaldan embraced the cross with joy. Abdul Waheed found no difficulty whatsoever. Rafiq and I were getting on so well, but then we encountered the cross. "The Qur'an says that Jesus didn't die," he said, smiling. And for the time being that was where it ended.

But the Qur'an at this point is wrong (Sura 4 v.146-149). The cross is history, both well-attested and well-documented.

However the work of the Holy Spirit is not restricted to the present. Part of our task is to present the Good News in a way that will allow our friends to process what they hear over future months and years.

Becoming a follower of Jesus

The idea that one is born a Muslim is deeply entrenched, and many of my Muslim friends have a very hard time understanding that you have to 'become a follower of Jesus'; though the idea that a non-Muslim can become one is not unfamiliar.

Westerners may be ethnic or cultural Christians and are often labelled as such, even though they may be secular atheist twenty-first century men and women. We encountered this problem in the first chapter. Ahmed came to England believing that all English people are Christians in the same way that most Arabs are Muslims. This is not an exaggeration; it is a view that prevails and results in Muslim men and women being shocked at what they see as the behaviour of Christians. They are mystified, outraged and confirmed in their initial opinion that Christianity is a religion of licence where drunkenness and prostitution are permitted. "But England is a Christian country," Ahmed will say. Not so. He needs a careful explanation. He needs to be introduced to the secular country that Britain has now become, and he needs us to explain that you become a Christian - you are never born one.

So how do you become a follower of Jesus?

Over coffee, a young Sudanese taxi driver was diligently trying to convert me to Islam. In the course of conversation I was unwise enough to quote the shehada: "Laa Illah illa illah." "Praise God!" he exclaimed, jumping to his feet, "you have become a Muslim!"

It took me sometime extricate myself from this and to explain that this was far from the case, but it was borne in on me that one had only to recite the shehada, "There is no God but Allah and Muhammad is his Prophet" to become a Muslim. Here is a form of words that in a kind of magical way makes one a Muslim. Our task is to show that becoming a disciple of Jesus is not magical, but involves a very earthy, practical and radical change of life.

"Follow me, and I will make you fishermen of men." (Mark ch.1 v.17).

This, Jesus' own call, includes:

The centrality of Jesus. 'Follow me'; not a set of rules or principles, not a set of religious observances, not even a set of beliefs, but me. This is set in direct contrast to religious observance and obedience to any set of laws. The rich young man (Matthew ch.19 v.16-22) said 'no' to Jesus, who had made it plain to him that all his religion, his attention to keeping the law and his doing good was irrelevant. We need to make this clear to our Muslim friends, many of whom will set great store by both religious rituals and the observance of the law as they see it. They will find it shocking and revolutionary.

Jesus taking the initiative. He calls; we respond. A conscious decision is demanded of us, to follow or to remain where we are. The rich young man stayed where he was. Peter, Matthew, James and John got up and followed Jesus.

The importance of continuing to follow. This is made clear by the narrative. Men and women followed Jesus physically as well as believing in him. Some stayed with him. Some left.

Saying yes to a new job offer. The call to us to become 'fishermen of men and women' is played out in the ongoing narrative of the New Testament. Fishing is an inspired metaphor, as it was - and still is - an industry involving a whole galaxy of skills: marketing, transport, rowing, sailing, boat-building and -repairing, net-making and other equipment construction and maintenance tasks, as well as actually sailing and catching fish. It is hard work; exciting, dangerous, fun, boring and uncomfortable by turns. It demands courage, endurance, patience and teamwork. Just look at the fishing narratives in the Gospels. Jesus calls us to any one of an infinite variety of tasks requiring many skills and personal qualities, all of which we need to develop. But Jesus' followers did not only have a new job; something amazing and wonderful happened to them. They were filled with the Holy Spirit! He will be the one who makes them fishermen for men and women. So you will explain to your Muslim friend that just as he or she will never become a follower of the Messiah by following rules or being religious, so they will not live their lives that way either. Instead, what you're talking about is nothing less than a real encounter with God that will be worked out in their normal daily lives.

Repentance

As well as the 'follow me' invitation and command, Jesus calls us to turn our backs on our old life and turn to God. Too easy? Look at the story of the lost son, the reprobate prodigal. The depths to which this young man fell are forcibly driven home to any Muslim, who reads with disgust that the boy actually went to look after pigs. How low can you get? Then he comes to his senses. He decides to go to his father and make a clean breast of it. No 'buts', no excuses. "I have done wrong against you and against God," he is ready to say. This is real repentance, admitting that you have done the worst thing imaginable. Not easy.

Much is often made of the importance being sorry for the wrongs we have done, and for the good we might have done and have failed to do. But look - there is nothing about being sorry here. The young man repents not because he is sorry but because he wants to survive. Always the realist, the rescuer Messiah is there for those who want to live and not die. Repentance is for survival. Sorrow, when we know God a bit better, may come later.

Men and women come to Christ in a million different ways. There is a glorious diversity in the work of the Holy Spirit. Many times he uses dreams and visions. Hamoud, my language teacher in Sudan, told me that over the course of two years or so he had dreamed over 200 dreams in which Jesus had spoken to him in different ways. What had finally moved and shaken him? The final dream, in which Jesus remonstrated with him. After so many dreams he had done absolutely nothing and he wasn't going to have any more dreams! Men and women come slowly or quickly to Jesus, and in many different ways, but there is always, in the end, a choice. It is always "follow me," in one form or another, and there is always, ultimately, repentance. "I came to follow Jesus when I was twenty-six," said Faisal, "and when I was thirty, I repented!"

What comes next is worked out in a kaleidoscope of different ways, but it involves a variation of what the disciples themselves experienced. Being with Jesus, being with his people, learning painfully, making a lot of mistakes (and often making a fool of oneself), having a lot of fun, sometimes finding ourselves in danger, sometimes finding ourselves exhilarated at the work of God, always experiencing the extraordinary relationships that Jesus' followers have with each other, and the conflict and heartbreak that so often come with them. Above all, being with Jesus and growing into a relationship with him. And experiencing a change in life at a deep level, whether slow or quick. Not at all what my taxi driver friend was thinking!

Judgement, Heaven and Hell

Is this the Good News? Yes it is. There is a sting in the tail; there are parts of the Good News that are bad news, and we will not be doing a favour to our Muslim friends if we ignore them. The rich young man whom Jesus looked on and loved, and invited to follow him, said no. What became of him?

Our Muslim friends will have a clear concept of the judgement of God, and its consequences. However, as we have seen earlier, we are at once on dangerous ground. We are using language that is common to us both, but do we mean the same things? Judgement and our ultimate fate are vital parts of the Good News. It has been said that Jesus, the one who alone can save us from Hell, talked most about it.[20]

What comes into the mind of your Muslim friend when you talk of these things? A Birmingham lady tells me that there are two angels with you, one on each shoulder. At the judgement the two angels will give an account, one of the good things you have said and done, and one of the bad. She tells me that one must not say anything in the toilet, because the angels, in their modesty, will not go in but will wait for you outside. This, and the caprice of God that Ahmed so clearly speaks of, are part of the perspectives on the judgement of God that you might hear. And you will be able to offer a Christian perspective in return; that the judgement of God, like everything else God does, is an expression of his perfect character, linked to his loving kindness, mercy and truth. It is the working-out of his anger against sin in human experience, and is integrally linked

[20] Leon Morris, "The Dreadful Harvest", *Christianity Today,* May 27, 1991
D. A. Carson. Jesus' Sermon on the Mount and His Confrontation with the World: An Exposition of Matthew 5-10 1 Apr 2004

to his own rescue plan. It is a truly terrifying prospect, and it is quite in order to gently and respectfully warn your friends that no human being can stand up and justify him or herself in the sight of God, and only God himself can enable you to survive the judgement. "Now I have discovered," said Abd al Waheed thoughtfully, "that there is nothing at all I can do to make myself acceptable to Allah."

No good deeds, piety, fasting, prayer or visits to Mecca can be of the slightest use. We cannot earn our way through the judgement of God. The parable of the tax collector and the Pharisee (or the bishop, or the imam) says it all. It is the mercy and grace of God, and our acknowledgment of our wickedness, that saves us; to rely on anything else is to be absolutely separated from the love and kindness of God forever.

Your Muslim friend may tell you, with justification, that the sensual view of Heaven given in the Qur'an is allegorical, and this is entirely justified. However, there is a dimension that, however allegorical or 'real' the image, is not present.- God himself. In the Qur'an, God is not present with his people in Heaven.

Our own good news is that God has a future for his people that is beyond understanding, and that that future starts now! The goodness and generosity of God the Father is expressed in the extravagant hospitality of his messianic banquet as he celebrates the victory and kingship of his son in the presence of the myriad men, women and children who have gratefully climbed onboard the rescue-craft created by his son Jesus. God himself is supremely and absolutely present at the feast, and his people will be present to him in an intimately close and loving relationship. The parable of the wedding feast (Matthew ch.22 v.1-14) illustrates the generosity of the king. In the story of the Prodigal Son (Luke ch.15 v.11-32). Jesus highlights the quite unreasonable profligacy of the father on the return of a son who deserves nothing but contempt. Jesus himself demonstrates the overwhelming generosity of his own father in providing wine and bread vastly in excess of what is needed.

God has a present for us as well as a future. Jesus tells parable after parable about the Kingdom of God, a dimension which is entirely absent in Islam, and which contrasts with the kingdom of Islam, which is Islamic rule on earth. The Kingdom of God is a kingdom in which we share during the present time, with all those who are coming into it. Here is a people who have the most extraordinary rights, privileges, joys and trials, as well as having a different life to live, a task to perform, and a struggle to engage in - all with the presence of the Holy Spirit to walk alongside us.

To set at liberty those who are oppressed

Jesus' Nazareth manifesto ("To set at liberty those who are oppressed...", Luke ch.4 v.18) plunges the Good News irretrievably into public life. Most of our Muslim friends come from cultures and countries where there is deeply-ingrained injustice, oppression and corruption; many will be asylum seekers, and will have suffered this at first hand. Some will have been oppressors themselves and have benefitted from it. Politics is a huge part of the Islamic biosphere, and even Muslims living outside the Muslim world are passionately involved in the politics of their country of origin. A rescue programme that does not have something to say about burning issues such as Palestine, Syria, Iraq, Azad Kashmir, and Kurdistan, does not meet the heart needs of the Muslim. Closer to home we need to assure oppressed and downtrodden people in Muslim communities in our own country that God cares about them. Jesus' words in the Nazareth synagogue express a theme that is constant throughout the Old Testament. "I have indeed seen the misery of my people in Egypt...and am concerned about their suffering," (Exodus ch.3 v.7). God is deeply concerned with the poor, the orphan, the refugee, the oppressed, the prisoner (whether guilty of crime or not), the powerless, and those subject to injustice. The narrative of the book of Exodus is good news for those living under oppressive regimes as it unfolds the story of God rescuing his people from slavery. We must never be afraid of encouraging our Muslim friends to speak of these matters, or of telling them the good news that Issa the Messiah is on the side of the oppressed and the poor, and that an essential component of God's judgement is bringing justice for the oppressed. Nor must we hold back this news from the rich, for whom it may be much less welcome.

Family

Very early on in the intoxicating days of the early Church, Peter is sent - most unwillingly - to a family of gentiles (Acts ch.10). A Jew to the tips of his fingers, even after three years in Jesus' company Peter has a hard time taking in the fact that God's rescue service is for all men and women, not just his own people. When we as Westerners read this story, we do not usually have problems with the Gentile-Jew axis, but we struggle with something that did not worry Peter at all. How can a whole family become Christians at once?

We have such an individual way of looking at God's dealings with us, and often we are forced to follow a very individual route with our Muslim friends because interest in the Good News can be so dangerous and highly-charged; but as we have seen earlier, in most Muslim cultures, the family is hugely powerful. It is often hard or impossible for people to escape the gravitational pull of their family. While as autonomous Western people we make our own individual decisions, it is hard for a member of a family with Asian heritage living in the West to make major decisions on their own, especially young people, and especially women. But as things change and families become more liberal, let us be wide open to the opportunity of sharing the Good News in a family context. This allows much good homework to go on while you are not there with them.

Conclusion

You will notice that I have used stories and quotations from the Gospels to make my argument here. This is because Paul's letters, useful as they are, are written for Christians. Jesus' words, for the most part, are addressed to unbelievers. In addition, it seems that the mindset and culture of Jesus' hearers might be closer to the Muslim mindset, though I would not want to generalise too much. But I also want to make the point that the Good News of God's rescue service is well communicated by the stories, miracles, words and life of Jesus alone.

There is also a heart dimension to this. Paul I respect, but Jesus I love! I want to hear him - the rescuer - speak his own good news.

I have also used incidents from daily life, and stories from within and outside Islamic culture, as illustrations. These link the Gospel to daily life and experience and take it out of the realm of the 'religious'. As Islam tends to be very religious, we need to offer a contrast, and offer a rescue service that is rooted in secular daily life. God is not religious; why should I be?

So let us speak the word of Jesus to those who will hear; and not quietly and soberly only, but with the passion that we feel, with gratefulness for what we have experienced, with anxiety for those who may be lost, with wonder at what God has done, and with the thrill of knowing we are talking about a truly amazing message.

Chapter 15

How can I know?

"We can't know whether we will go to Heaven or to Hell."

We have returned to this, very common, belief on a number of occasions and it is a vitally important part of the Good News. How can I know where I stand with God? As always, rather than supplying a ready answer, we should ask why the question is being asked in the first place, though it is itself perhaps one of the most pressing existential questions that one can ever ask.

Put loosely, many of my Muslim friends feel that if they pray, do the pilgrimage, and carry out other 'acts of piety', they will have a better chance of getting to Heaven - not that they think about it very much, but they believe, broadly, that if they do 'good things' they stand a better chance.

But Amjad, an intelligent young businessman in Port Sudan, said to me, "You can't know what God is going to do with you! You might have lived a great life, been terribly religious and done loads of good things...and God might still send you to Hell. You might only have done one good thing in your life, and God might send you to Heaven! God has perfect freedom to do what he likes with you and me at any time."

Here is the caprice of the Islamic God perfectly described. But the God we know is not capricious. We can know where we are with him. He is reliable. It is tempting to say that God, being absolutely free to do what he wishes, has yet said that he will behave towards us in a certain way; but that would not be true. God is actually not free to act outside the constraints of his own character. God has made a covenant with his people and that covenant, like his law, his creation, his Gospel and his son himself, is an expression of what he is like.

What is a covenant? An agreement, a kind of contract - but certainly not one that is entered into equally and freely. It is an agreement imposed by the powerful on the powerless. God's covenant is imposed by him on his own people. In it, God states how he will behave towards the people, and how they will behave towards him. A theme that runs through the Bible is the constant failure of the covenants between God and his people due to the inability of God's people to remain faithful to the conditions that have been laid down. There are repeated covenants, the last one being the new covenant established by Jesus. The constant problem of God's people and their unwillingness and inability to remain faithful is solved by Jesus, by Issa the Messiah himself, who fulfils the letter and spirit of the covenant on both sides - God's side and ours. It is important that we talk about this covenant with our Muslim friends because it clearly demonstrates the faithful and reliable nature of the Christian God, just as the absolute freedom of the God of Islam to do what he chooses at any time demonstrates his capricious nature. They are, in this sense anyway, opposites. When there is no covenant there is no commitment from God that he will behave in a certain way. We cannot know what he is going to do next. Those in the hands of the God of Islam cannot possibly know what he will do with them. For the Christian, being within the covenant relationship is to be safe in God's hands. It is to have passed from death to life. It is to know where we stand with him.

There is covenant, and then there is relationship. We have seen earlier how this idea is also absent in Islam. God does not relate to his people. He does not love them in the way that Christians understand. As my student friend said, "God is above that kind of thing."

He isn't!

A familiar sight at about 4pm in Jordan is of children coming home from school. Girls in their green tunics and white headscarves walking five abreast, arm in arm, oblivious of the traffic. Little boys, rucksacks flying over their shoulders as they run home. One breaks off from the group, runs up to a door and bangs with all his might. "Mama, Mama. I'm home. Let me in!"

Does this little boy think even for a moment that the door will be shut against him? Of course not - but why not? Let your friends think for a moment. The little boy is family. He is their boy. He has a right to go in because he lives there and it is his home. He trusts in the relationship without thinking. Any other child will knock politely, and not know what the answer will be - maybe it's "come in!" and maybe he will be sent packing. He does not know because he does not have the relationship. He is not family.

This picture may shock your Muslim friend, but God is like that: as his children, bought by his own rescuer the Messiah Issa, we are welcome; we even - dare we say it - have rights there. We have a home. And we have all this because of the relationship that God has brought us into. We are family.

Reading the Bible together will enable you to show your friend that God has a deep and powerful love for his people. More than that, it will show them that love is central to his character. Love is what God is! Without love there can be no relationship, but relationship is what God desires to have with his people.

Postscript

"What did you do at the battle of Waterloo, Grandpa?" the grandchildren ask. "Well," says Grandpa, "I didn't seem to do much really. I stood in a line and I fired my musket a few times, but I have no idea whether I hit anything. We marched at a great pace from one place to another and then back again to where we started, but I am not quite sure why. There was a lot of noise and shouting, and sometimes I was scared. But we won the battle."

Grandpa might think that the battle could have just as easily been won without him, but he would be wrong. He played his part just like thousands of others. Many played a modest part, but every part that was played was indispensible.

I feel like Grandpa. My wife and I have been in a long campaign that is going to be won and, in some funny way, we have had something to do with it, but I can't point to anything concrete. But we have been part of a great company of servants, one that has existed for centuries, and will continue to exist into the future. There are countless men and women in it. A very few of them I know well; most are entirely unknown to me.

If you have managed to read this far you will see that I have offered no magic formulae, but just a few useful lessons that I have learned the hard way, and a few mistakes to avoid.

Hassan was farming his goats and caring for his ancient olive trees in the achingly beautiful hills of northern Jordan.

"You haven't done too well for rain this year," I said. It was April. The dry ground should have been a riot of grass and wild flowers.

"The grass should be up to here," Hassan bangs his knee with his big square hand. "There's hardly enough for the animals." Then he reaches up and gently pulls down the branch of an olive tree. "But look at this!" he smiles, as he points to a mass of tiny green bumps. "The olive harvest is going to be terrific!"

The New Testament is full of farming metaphors. However brilliant Hassan is, he does not expect to produce any olives before November. It is still six months until the time when he and every member of his family will drop everything and spend three weeks picking olives. As Christians, we are in the same situation.

A friend once remarked, "God's work comes in three phases; impossible, difficult and done." In our corner of God's workshop we seem to be at a very exciting phase; we are slowly moving from the impossible to the merely difficult. This fact rests on the faithfulness of countless men and women and the timing of God. It is a very thrilling time, and I hope to live to see the 'done' part. I have written mainly for those of us living in Western Europe; among Muslims from Iran there has been massive growth in God's Church, but among those from Pakistani heritage in the West the time has not yet come. Church history tells us to be confident that their time will come.

God, the master of history, uses huge secular forces to achieve his purposes and to bring the right time closer. The British Muslim culture that we looked at earlier is changing rapidly in response to these forces: the Islamic biosphere as it exists in our own country is responding to a variety of factors: the secularisation of the native culture and its education system, the exposure of Muslim intellectuals to new ideas and values through business, university and other areas of life, the emergence of a second and third generation whose culture diverges more and more from the culture from which their grandparents came, and countless other factors.

By contrast with this, there is a very high birth rate over the last two decades, which has resulted in communities whose sheer size militates against integration, and against individuals and families forming relationships with people from outside their community, and a sense of racism and 'otherness' - rightly or wrongly perceived - as well as a very strong rearguard action by the elderly and the uneducated whose agenda is to maintain the cultural status quo.

Overshadowing this is the very obvious and growing conflict, not to say outright civil war, within the Muslim world. We hear a great deal about 'radicalisation', but we hear little about the huge amount of internal work that is being done in the heads and hearts of many Muslims. "How can I, an intelligent and humane person, be part of this? Why does the Qur'an not tell me to how to live peaceably with my neighbours, but instead encourage enmity with the majority of people in my own country?"

This internal critique cannot be left to be a private affair within Islamic communities. Although the impetus must come from within Muslim communities, Westerners have a most important role to play. We need to make relationships, to have fun and enjoy normal life and work with our Muslim friends, asking pertinent questions and listening to the answers, letting them say things they cannot say within their own culture.

We need to challenge, and let them challenge, the comfortable illusion that the jihadists and the extremists practice a perverted form of Islam. "What is the defining difference between ISIS, Daesh, (or whatever you chose to call it), and your own true form of Islam?" is a vital question to ask. It is at least arguable that the warlike and fierce faith that jihadists practice is compatible with Islamic history, the life of the Prophet, and the words of the Qur'an.

No Muslim ever failed to get an invitation to the banquet of the King, or was ever lost because he or she was a Muslim. God is not even slightly interested in what religion we adhere to; whether we are secularists, atheists, postmodernists, evangelical Christians, Satanists or simply nothing at all. He is concerned only that we take full advantage of his rescue service; that we grab hold of what his son has done for us with both our hands. In God's sight we are all equally needy, all equally loved, and all equally redeemable.

Appendix

Questions for Muslims

This list gives an idea of the huge variety of questions that you might ask. Some you will find useful, some not. I have settled for just a tiny handful.

Three favourites:

When you die, are you going to Heaven or to Hell?

What is God like?

What does God think about you?

About Islam:

What is God like?

What does Islam/the Prophet/the Qur'an say about God's love?

By what authority does the Prophet Muhammad speak?

How do we know that the Prophet and the Qur'an are from God?

When did God speak directly to the Prophet (i.e. not via the angel Gabriel)?

What miracles did the Prophet do?

Who, apart from the Prophet, saw the angel Gabriel?

Who saw the Prophet go on his miraculous journey on the night of power?

What are the signs of a prophet?

How do we know that the angel Gabriel came from God? (i.e. that it was the angel Gabriel who spoke to Muhammad).

What was the relationship between God and the Prophet like?

How does God show mercy and justice at the same time?

Have you ever considered that Islam might not be true?

Why does Islam have the death penalty for those who leave Islam?

About Jesus:

What do you know about Jesus?

Where is the tomb of the Prophet? Where is the tomb of Jesus the Messiah?

Muslims are commanded to respect Jesus. What in practical terms might this mean? (Might it mean reading the Bible? Finding out more about him? Any other thing?)

Who is the father of Jesus Christ?

What does the Qur'an say about Jesus? (Sura 3.v.45 et sec)

Who and what is the Messiah?

About Christianity:

What do you think Christians believe?

Why have Muslims changed the Bible? (Yes - why have the Bible passages quoted in the Qur'an been changed?)

Why are Muslims so afraid of the Bible or Bible translation?

Why are churches special targets in Muslim countries?

Why are churches not allowed to exist in some Muslim countries?

Why are there so many Muslim countries where Christians are persecuted?

Why is there no death penalty for Christians who leave Christianity?

Why does Islam still have the death penalty for Muslim men, and severe sanctions for women, who leave Islam for another faith?

About you, a Muslim:

When you die, will you go to Heaven or to Hell?

What does God think of you?

What does God feel about you?

How have you experienced God today?

Islam proclaims that God is merciful. How has God shown his mercy to you?

About me, a non-Muslim:

What does God think of me?

How can God forgive me?

Where do I stand before God as far as judgement is concerned?

What is your attitude to me in the light of the above?

Sura 9 in the Qur'an has a number of verses that say that Muslims should wage war on unbelievers. What do you feel about this?

As a Muslim, what good news do you have for me, a non-Muslim?

Others:

Can a person love God?

What are people who want to follow God meant to be like in character?

How can the Muslim community bless the country?

What is more important for an oppressed people, jihad or acts of compassion?

Why do Muslims not speak out against Muslim tyrants and evil governments?

Notes: some of these questions are obviously loaded. You may want to alter the way they are asked so that they do not appear too threatening, though some are meant to be.

Questions are not:

> To score a point.

> To win an argument.

> To obtain an answer!

Questions are:

> To encourage dialogue.

> A friendly way of bringing up difficult subjects.

> To make people think.

Don't press for an answer; in fact, encourage people not to answer but to think about the matter you have raised.

Don't immediately answer the question if your friend cannot find an answer to a question you have asked.

Top 10 Books

If you can't face the long reading list, read these first!

Jens Christensen, *The Practical Approach to Muslims* (North Africa Mission, 1977)

Thabiti Anyabwile, *The Gospel for Muslims* (Moody Publishers, 2010)

Samy Tanagho, *Glad News! God Loves You, My Muslim Friend* (Authentic, 2003)

Ali Dashti, *23 Years: A Study of the Prophetic Career of Mohammad* (Mazda Publishers, 1944)

Robert Scott, *Dear Abdullah: Eight Questions Muslim People Ask About Christianity* (IVP, 2011)

Martin Goldsmith, *Beyond Beards and Burqas; Connecting With Muslims* (IVP, 2009)

Ibn Warraq, *Why I am not a Muslim* (Prometheus Books, 2003)

Caroline Cox and John Marks, *The West, Islam and Islamism* (Civitas, 2003)

Greg Koukl, *Tactics, A Game Plan for Discussing Your Christian Convictions* (Grand Rapids: Zondervan, 2009)

Robin Fisher, *Change and Stability in an Urban Muslim Society* (M.Phil thesis, Birmingham University, 1997)

Bibliography

Abdul Rauf, Muhammad; *Islamic View of Women and the Family* (New York: Robert Speller and Sons, 1976)

Ahmad, Imtiaz, ed.; *Ritual and religion among Muslims in India* (New Delhi: Manohar, 1981)

Ahmad, Imtiaz, ed.; *Family, Kinship and Marriage among Muslims in India* (New Delhi: Manohar, 1979)

Ahmed, Leila; *Women and Gender in Islam* (Newhaven and London: Yale University Press, 1992)

Anwar, Mohammed; *The Myth of Return: Pakistanis in Britain* (London: Heinemann, 1979)

Atiya, Nayra; *Khul-Khaal: Five Egyptian Women Tell Their Stories* (Syracuse University Press, 1992)

Ardener, Shirley; *Women and Space; Ground Rules and Social Maps* (Oxford: Berg Publishers, 1993)

Asenda, Georgio; *Leisurely Nomads: the Hadendowa of the Gash Delta* (Ann Arbor: UMI, 1987)

Azari, Farah; *Women of Iran* (London: Ithaca Press, 1993)

Badran, Margot; *Feminists, Islam and Nation* (Princeton: Princeton Universty Press, 1994)

Baldick, Julian; *Mystical Islam* (London: I B. Tauris, 1989)

Ballard, Roger, ed.; *Desh Pardesh: The South Asian Presence in Britain* (London: Hurst and Company, 1994)

Bucaille, Maurice; *The Bible, the Qur'an and Science* (English Edition - Indianapolis: American Trust Publications, 1979)

Bulliet, Richard; *Islam, the View from the Edge* (New York: Columbia University Press, 1994)

Beck, Lois and Keddie, Nikki; *Women in the Muslim World* (Cambridge, Mass: Harvard University Press, 1978)

Darsh, Dr S.M.; *Muslims in Europe* (London: Ta Ha Publishers, 1980)

Von Denfer, Dietrich; *"Baraka as a Basic Concept of Muslim Belief"* (Islamic Studies vol. xv, no.3, 1976)

Donaldson, Bess; *The Wild Rue, a Study of Muhammedan Magic and Folklore in Iran* (London: Luzac and Co., 1938)

Donnan, Hastings; *Marriage among Muslims: Preference and Choice in Northern Pakistan* (Delhi: Hindustan Publishing Corporation; Leiden: EJ Brill, 1988)

Douglas, Mary; *Purity and Danger* (London: Routledge, 1966)

Douglas, Mary; *Natural Symbols* (London: Barrie and Rockliff, The Cresset Press, 1970)

Dundes, Alan; *The Evil Eye* (Wisconsin: University of Wisconsin Press, 1992)

Evans-Pritchard. E. E.; *Social Anthropology* (Cohen and West, 1951)

Geaves, Ron; *Sectarian Influences Within Islam in Britain* (Dept. of Theology and Religious Studies, University of Leeds, 1996)

Geijbels, M; *"Aspects of the Veneration of the Saints in Islam, with Special Reference to Pakistan"* (Moslem World, vol. 68, 1978)

Geijbels, M.; *Muslim Festivals and Ceremonies in Pakistan* (Rawalpindi: Christian Study Centre, 1982)

Gerholme, Tomas and Lithman, Yngve; *The New Islamic presence in Western Europe* (London: Mansell, 1988)

Gidoomal, Ram; *Sari n' Chips* (MARC, 1993)

Gilsenan, Michael; *Recognising Islam* (London and Canberra: Croom Helm, undated)

Grunland, Stephen A.; *Cultural Anthropology, a Christian Perspective.* (Grand Rapids: Zondervan, 1979)

Haviland, William A.; *Cultural Anthropology* (London, New York: Harcourt Brace Jovanovich, College Publishers, 1990)

Henley, Alix; *Asians in Britain: Caring for Muslims and their Families: Religious Aspects of Care* (Cambridge: DSS, 1982)

Hickey, Gary; *Primary Health Care in the Inner City: a Study into Primary Health Care in Sparkbrook and Sparkhill* (Birmingham: South Birmingham Community Health Council, 1992)

Hopkins, Nicholas and Saad Edin, Ibrahim; *Arab Society: Social Science Perspectives* (Cairo: American University Press, 1985)

Hussain, Asaf; *The Educated Pakistani Girl* (Karachi: Ima Printers, 1963)

Iliff, Frances P.; *Understanding Muslim Culture* (London: Interserve, M.A.B., 1994)

Irving, T.B. and Ahsan, Muhammad; *The Qur'an, Basic Teachings* (Leicester: Ahmad, Khurshid, Islamic Foundation, 1979)

Jackson, John A.; *Migration* (Longman, 1966)

Jeffery, Patricia; *Migrants and Refugees* (Cambridge: C.U.P., 1976)

Jones, Bevan; *Women in Islam* (Lucknow Publishing House, 1941)

Kannan, C.T.; *Cultural Adaptation of Asian Immigrants* (Bombay: India Printing Works, 1978)

Kaseras, P. and Hopkins, E.; *British Asians Health in the Community* (Chichester: Wiley and Sons, 1987)

Krausz, Ernest; *Ethnic Minorities in Britain* (London: MacGibbon and Kee Ltd., 1971)

Lewis, Philip; *Pirs, Shrines and Pakistani Islam* (Rawalpindi: Christian Study Centre)

Lewis, Philip; *Islamic Britain* (London: I.B. Tauris, 1994)

Lichtenstäder, I.; *Women in the Aiyim al Arab* (London: The Royal Asiatic Society, 1935)

Lings, Martin; *What is Sufism?* (London: Allen and Unwin, 1975)

Maus, Marcel; *A General Theory of Magic* (London and Boston: Routlege and Keegan Paul, 1950)

Mackey, Sandra; *The Saudis: Inside the Desert Kingdom* (New York: Meridian, 1987)

Malinowski, Bronislaw; *Magic, Science and Religion, and Other Essays* (Souvenir Press, 1948)

Marsot, Afaf; *Society and the Sexes in Mediaeval Islam* (Malibu: Undena Publications, 1979)

Maududi, A.A.; *Towards Understanding Islam* (Lahore: Idara Tarjuman ul Quran, 1960)

McCurry, Don M. ed.; *The Gospel and Islam: a 1978 Compendium. The Papers and Research of the North American Conference on Muslim Evangelism* (California: MARC, 1978)

Mernissi, Fatima; *Beyond the Veil* (London: Al Saqi books, 1985)

Mernissi, Fatima; *The Harem Within* (London; Doubleday, 1994)

Mernissi, Fatima; *Women and Islam* (Oxford: Blackwell, 1991)

Mernissi, Fatima; *Women's Rebellion and Islamic Memory* (London: Zed Books Ltd, 1996)

Morris, Brian; *Anthropological Studies of Religion* (London: CUP, 1987)

Mosteshar, Cherry; *Unveiled* (London: Hodder and Stoughton, 1995)

Muhsen, Zana; *Sold* (London: Warner Books, 1991)

Musk, Bill; *The Unseen Face of Islam* (MARC, 1989)

Murphy, Robert E.; *The Dialectics of Social Life* (New York: Basic Books Inc., 1971)

Mutahhari, Murtada; *The Rights of Women in Islam* (Tehran: WOFIS, 1981)

Nadwi, A.; *Islamic Concept of Prophethood* (Lucknow: Academy of Islamic Research and Publications, undated)

Nielsen. J.; *Muslims in Western Europe* (Edinburgh University Press, 1992)

North, C.W.; *Islam in Schools and Madrassahs; a Field Study in Sparkbrook, Sparkhill and Small Heath* (Birmingham: University of Birmingham, C.S.I.C. 1983, 1985; M.A. 1986)

Owen, David; *"South Asian People in Britain, Social and Economic Circumstances"* 1991 Census Statistical paper no.7 ESRC (University of Warwick: Centre for Research in Ethnic Relations, 1994)

Parshall, Phil.; *Bridges to Islam* (Grand Rapids: Baker, 1983)

Qur'an, Text and Commentary; Translation by Abdulla Yusif Ali (Jeddah: Islamic Education Centre, 1946)

Qureshi, Bashir; *Transcultural Medicine* (Lancaster: Kluwer Academic Publishers, 1989)

Ram, Monder; *"Workplace Relations in Ethnic Minority Firms in the West Midland Clothing Industry"* (New Community, 19/4, July 1993)

Rippin, Andrew; *Muslims: Their Religious Beliefs and Practices, vol.ii, The Contemporary Period* (Routledge, 1993)

Robertson Smith, W.; *Kinship and Marriage in Early Arabia* (London: Darf, 1990. 1st edn. 1885)

Roy, Shibani; *Status of Muslim Women in North India* (Delhi: B.R. Publishing Corporation, 1979)

Rule, Babs; *Everyday Life in the Harem* (London: W.H Allen and Co., 1986)

Saadawi, Nawal; *The Hidden Face of Eve* (London: Zed Books, 1980)

Saifullah Khan, V.; *"The Pakistanis: Mirpuri Villagers at Home and in Bradford"*, ch.3 in J. Watson, ed., *Between Two Cultures* (Oxford: Blackwell, 1977)

Saifullah Khan, V. ed.; *Minority Families in Britain: Support and Stress* (London: Macmillan, 1979)

Saifullah Khan, V.; *"Pakistani Women in Bradford"*, (New Community, vol. V, no. 12, 1976)

Shafi, Mufti Mohammed; *The Life of the Last Prophet* (New Delhi: Islamic Book Foundation, 1987)

Shaw, Alison; *A Pakistani Community in Britain* (Oxford: Blackwell, 1988)

Schimmel, Annemarie; *Mystical Dimensions of Islam* (London: the University of North Carolina Press, 1970)

Schimmel, Annemarie; *Islam, an Introduction* (State University of New York Press, 1992)

Schimmel, Annemarie; *And Muhammed is his Messenger* (Chapel Hill and London: University of North Carolina Press, 1985)

Siddiqi, Mohammad; *Women in Islam* (Lahore: Institute of Islamic Culture, 1966)

Smith, R. Cantwell; *The Meaning and End of Religion* (London: SPCK, 1962)

Tahir Rasool Qadri; *"Hadith of Marriage"* (The Universal Message, Jan. 1982)

Thanawi, A.A. Molana; *Perfecting Women, Bihishti Zewar*. tr. Barbara Daly Metcalf (Berkeley, California: 1990)

Turner, Victor; *The Ritual Process* (London: Routledge and Keegan Paul, 1969)

Troll, Christian; *Shrines and Sufis of Byapur, 1300-1700* (Princeton: U.V.P.)

Troll, Christian; *Muslim Shrines in India* (Delhi: O.U.P., 1992)

UN Department of Economic & Social Affairs; *Human Settlements, The Environmental Challenge* (Macmillan, 1992)

Utas, Bo.; *Women in Islamic Societies* (SIAS: Curzon Press, 1983)

Van Baal, Jan.; *Symbols for Communication* (Assen: Van Gorcum, 1971)

Vreeda de Stuers, C., *Parda. A Study of Muslim Women's Life in Northern India* (Assen: Van Gorcum, 1968)

Wallis Budge, Sir E.A.; *Amulets and Superstitions* (Oxford: OUP, 1930)

Watson, James, ed.; *Between Two Cultures* (Oxford: Blackwell, 1977)

Wehr, Hans; *Dictionary of Modern Written Arabic* (Beirut: Librarie du Liban,1974)

Werbner, Pnina; *The Migration Process* (New York, Berg, 1990)

Werbner, Pnina; *"Stamping the Earth with the Name of Allah; Zikr and the Sacralising of Space Among British Muslims"* (unpublished paper, University of Manchester, 1990)

Walvin, James; *Black Ivory: A History of British Slavery* (London: HarperCollins, 1992)

Westermarck, Edward; *Pagan Survivals in Mohammedan Civilisation* (London: Macmillan, 1933)